Anjali Deshpande is a journalist and activist. She has participated in many campaigns and movements including the women's movement and the Bhopal gas tragedy survivors' struggle for justice. A bilingual author who writes in both English and Hindi, Deshpande's first novel in English—*Impeachment*, was published in 2012, and was recreated in Hindi as *Mahabhiyog*, in 2016. She has, under her belt, a collection of short-stories in Hindi, *Ansari ki maut ki Ajeeb Dastaan* (2019), and a Hindi novella, *Hatya* (2019), which has been translated into German under the title *Mord* (2023). Deshpande has also co-authored *Factory Japani, Pratirodh Hindustani* (2023) with Nandita Haksar, translated into English as *Japanese Management, Indian Resistance* (2023).

NOBODY LIGHTS A CANDLE

Anjali Deshpande

SPEAKING TIGER

SPEAKING TIGER BOOKS LLP
125A, Ground Floor, Shahpur Jat, near Asiad Village,
New Delhi 110049

First published in Hindi as *Hatya* by Rajpal and Sons in 2019
First published in English by Speaking Tiger Books in 2024

ISBN: 978-93-5447-936-6
eISBN: 978-93-5447-749-2

10 9 8 7 6 5 4 3 2 1

Typeset in ArnhemFine by SÜRYA, New Delhi
Printed at HT Media Ltd, Greater Noida

To my partner
Anand Kumar
who introduced me to the reality of caste
and did not live to see the English version

1

Morning again. The trumpeting of a bus hurtling past his house broadcast the news and the noisy clanking of iron poles dropping one on top of another onto the back of a tempo confirmed it. Adhirath guessed that the tent supplier's family, who lived across the narrow lane, was about to bring home another thick wad of currency notes. 'How much money people have begun to make,' he thought, still lying abed, 'they splurge on parties, engagements, weddings, naming a newborn, birthdays and anniversaries; tents keep springing up everywhere.'

A few rags of sunlight wormed their way through the thick armour of dust on the pane of the window that was never opened, and settled beside him. The sun always finds a way to announce the morning, even in this age when streetlamps and inverter-ridden houses had swallowed the stars. One could only tell it was night because the noise levels went down a bit. Now that he came to think if it, the difference between day and night, the very passage of time had become meaningless in any practical sense in his life. Still the sun made him aware that another day had arrived. Yes, morning again. Time to get up and face the world for a few hours, a world that had kept shrinking around him in the last few months.

He got up, slowly pushing the khes towards his ankles.

Could the world not wait? This was the day after Holi, the spring festival. Surely, everyone had the right to take their time. He began to move more slowly, imagining himself in a slow-motion film as he stood up. He stretched his arms above his head with the same deferential languor. And with that, he had done all that he needed to do for the morning. He dragged himself out of the room to go down the stairs. His mother stood outside the little stoop in front of the doorway, arguing with the vegetable seller.

'You know, in this season, peas are so cheap they are almost being distributed free, and you...'

'Ammaji, peas are on the way out, will they not extract a goodbye price? Fifty rupees for five kgs; that is the price in the mandi...'

Another iron pole clanged into place beside its peers in the back of the tempo. A motorcycle roared past, upbraiding people for being in its way. He opened the screen door to the house and banged it shut after him.

Inside, he walked through the doorway that had been cut into the partition, which divided the long room into two unequal portions. The portion behind the partition was longer and accommodated the fridge, a box bed and several metal trunks. A small toilet occupied the far end of the elongated room. Pushpa, his wife of eight years, stood at the kitchen counter in a sort of alcove defined by the washroom wall, rolling out chapattis with vehemence. As he turned on the tap in the wash basin next to the little loo, he noticed that her back remained stiff and resentful of his presence behind her. Because he had woken up late? She had obviously not had the time to start making his tea. He brushed his teeth, then gargled unnecessarily loudly and spat with gusto in the basin even as he cast sideways glances at her straight back. The back stiffened a little more, or so it seemed.

The hot tawa banged, a round roti nearly caught fire and was dumped rudely on the hot pile of its predecessors in the box. Steam billowed out of its stomach. Nothing would mellow that back. He decided to walk his son to school.

He took Varun's hand, pulling him off the box bed gently, then picked up his school bag.

'Mummy, bye,' said the child.

'I am going,' Adhirath said unnecessarily.

'Bye, beta, bye,' his wife said. The rolling pin kept moving.

For nearly a year now he had been bathing and dressing his son. Earlier his duties ended with finding a spot for Varun among twenty children in the school's Maruti van that picked him up at their doorstep. For two months now, he had been walking his son to school.

'We can save money on the van,' Pushpa had said. 'The school is just here.'

Six-year-old Varun did not like this new ritual. He went to and returned from school with his cheeks swollen in resentment. It was a fifteen-minute walk to Little Saints National Convent School. The child's sullen palm complained every day to his father's firm grip, about the loss of fifteen precious minutes of early morning sleep, or even just a doze, a restful doze nestling under the warmth of the quilt. Adhirath felt he had stolen that joy from his little son, even though he had been enjoying it himself for a year now. So why did he not feel rested today?

He returned on feet that seemed weighed down and stood at the door, looking around. More two-wheelers sped past, a car drove by, the driver's hand firmly on the horn. Adhirath hurled a string of abuses at the car and its driver. Then he went in and slumped on the sofa. In the floor-to-ceiling showcase that acted as the partition, a television commanded pride of place at the centre, a string of stuffed animals in improbable colours marching around it.

'Not a single gujhiya. Nothing,' his mother said to him as she handed him his cup of tea. 'Not for us but at least for the grandson, they could have sent half a kilo. How much does it cost? Not much. He is their grandson too. It is the same story every festival. We have never asked for anything but...'

'I have to leave,' Pushpa said, as she walked past. She had done her morning chores. The chapattis for breakfast were in the hotpot. The pressure cooker sat on the stove hissing malevolently about the daal and the potatoes. The counter was wiped clean. Pans, plates, grater, cups, ladles and other assorted dishes had been pushed to one side of the counter. Let others do the washing, how much could she do? He heard the rage in her clicking steps and sighed. She was going to bathe. To dress. To paint her lips, pick up her purse and stuff her mobile phone in it. To leave for office. Away from this house full of crabby people. She would do it as fast as she could, not spending a minute more than necessary in her home.

He stared at the camels, goats and tigers, chasing each other, behind the glass panes. They had picked them up in Agra nearly two years ago. How infernally crowded the town had been and how they had cursed everybody, for nobody had any clue where the Taj Mahal was. The glass case of the small replica of the Taj Mahal was cracked now. It sat above the animals. How long had it been since they had gone on a trip? He now used the motorcycle only occasionally. The car rarely moved from the side of the road where it was almost permanently parked. Pushpa had asked him to sell it. She said they couldn't afford the EMIs. And they were definitely not going out on a vacation in the car soon. He would sit here watching TV or eyeballing the plastic animals above it, listening to his father crib about cold rotis, watching his mother heat the vegetables, and his wife getting ready to go out and earn.

'Is this a roti? Nowadays women simply don't know how to knead flour,' his father was saying. 'I have seen my mother do it. Gathering up the flour from the paraat, adding the water gently, kneading it, punching it, spreading it out, folding it back in, giving it a punch here and a tuck there. They imagined the soft chapattis they would roll out and hummed a tune while they kneaded. They did all this with love. They worked hard, for they thought that they were cooking for their children, for their husbands, for people they loved. Now they think it a chore, they have no time to knead flour or roast the rotis properly. There are families who are now making do with baread bought from the market. Yes, baread. These women, they don't want to work... if only they spent half the time they spend on making up their faces on kneading flour, they would have no pains and aches in the joints. They think they are doing the world a favour by preening in front of the mirror...just look, look at this roti, it is so thick, like it is cardboard, uncooked in one part, burnt in another. Where are you, Adhir's mother, come here, you can't even make a few fresh rotis for your husband for breakfast?'

This was his cue. He called Nitesh, his batch mate, now posted in the Chhatarpur village police station. He had to get out, go as far as he could from the stiffening spine of his wife, his sobbing son and his crabby father.

'Bapu, I have to be away today. You get Varun from school,' he cut into his father's song of complaint, 'Get there by two, okay?'

He ran upstairs. Pushpa had already painted her lips. She picked up the damp towel from the back of the chair, spread it on the string outside, picked up her purse and walked out.

His mother talked of the rising cost of living, his father of Pushpa's reluctant performance of chores. And Pushpa turned her back on him and told him she was too tired to give him company in anything. Did half a salary make him half a man? She was always making him aware of his truncated income, aware of how the price of everything was going up. He shut the door behind her and had a bath.

He checked his wallet. Only a hundred rupees and some change. He would need petrol. Gone were the days when he could fill the tank without any thought of the price of fuel. Now he rarely got his tank filled. Two litres or three. That was enough. The motorcycle sat on the pavement, most of the time, idle like him.

He raced through the crowded lanes, dodging rickshaws, grazing one gleaming white car in the narrow street, and hurling abuse at the nattily dressed owner at the wheel. He felt good. It had been a long time since he had abused some well-dressed bugger lustily. He jumped a red light, although not deliberately; he had just forgotten to look at the signal. But he was sure he would not get a ticket had there even been a traffic cop on the kerb. Some perks of the job remain even if the job itself is in jeopardy, he told himself and relaxed again.

He arrived at the police station two hours later, tired by the drive, his back hurting, his inner thighs tight. He had grown unused to sitting astride the bike for so long. Come to think of it, he had not straddled anything in the last few weeks. He chuckled. Time to grip something between his legs. Otherwise, how could he feel like a man? He glanced at himself in the rearview mirror, combed his hair, stuffed the tiny comb back in his nearly empty wallet, parked the bike along the wall, and walked into the station, throwing a casual hello to the man behind the granite counter and steering left to the room where Nitesh should have been.

The room was empty.

The man from behind the counter had followed him.

'He left,' he said. 'He did not call you?'

Adhirath fished his mobile phone out of his pocket. Three missed calls. Two from Nitesh. One from his landline at home.

He used the desk phone to call home. His mother had called to ask if he would return for lunch.

'Why would I ask father to fetch Varun if I was going to return by noon?' he asked, a bit irritated.

'He never told me. You never told me. Nobody tells me anything. How would I know? You should tell me. I was about to make chapattis for lunch...would have made for you too. Who would have eaten them, tell me? I would have to eat them, stale chapattis, and they don't suit me anymore; does anyone care? My knees, they hurt so much...'

'You could throw them away,' he hissed.

'Do you even know the price of flour; it is twenty rupees a kilo at the mill...'

He banged down the phone and inhaled deeply. All this ruckus about chapattis that had not even been made yet.

'When did Nitesh say he will return?' he asked the constable who had taken his place behind the counter and was pretending he was not listening in on the conversation. 'Gone on a round?'

It seemed like a quiet morning, the calm of the day after a festival, the slightly drunk restfulness after the rowdy revelry of Holi. There was hardly any traffic on the road outside. The few shops across the road in the small local market looked empty. This was the kind of place where the police had little to do. This was one of those police stations that would not even be auctioned. Nobody would pay to be posted here. No source of income. Some people might have consumed ganja and got rowdy, but that was all. Lots of bloody rich folk, each living a kilometre away from the other in huge farmhouses; for the rest, the villagers, who sorted things out for themselves and beat up the police if they dared interfere. The police station looked empty.

'There has been a murder, Janaab. That is where they have gone,' said the constable.

Adhirath stared. Murder? In this sleepy place?

'Where?'

'We heard around nine o'clock. Past nine actually. The pradhan of Chandola village called. A woman murdered in a farmhouse.'

Adhirath hauled himself back on his black motorcycle. His thighs protested and he tried a friction massage on the seat. A truck went past with sheets of tin on its back, clanging a harsh note at him. The road ahead was empty except for the truck. Gurgaon and its malls were close by but he had no money to catch a movie. Even the movies were now out of reach for the poor. A single ticket would rob him of at least 150, maybe more, and they don't let you carry even a bottle of water inside. He could simply roam around, window shopping. He looked ahead at the inviting road. Under a peepul tree a knot of three men stood, smoking beedis. The cut in the divider where he would have to make a U-turn was near that tree. He gunned the motorcycle but drove slowly. Near the tree he stopped and beckoned one of the men. 'Which way is Chandola?' he asked.

'Go straight. You will come to a market. You keep going straight. Then you cross the railway line. Then you take a right turn. There will be a station. There you ask someone. It is not far.'

Adhirath let go of the clutch. Anyway there were no chapattis waiting for him at home.

He arrived at Jhandapur railway station, having stopped three more times to ask for directions. Only then it occurred to him that he had not bothered to ask in which farmhouse the murder had been committed. Adhirath surveyed the lie of the land and decided his best bet would be the market adjoining the station.

Surrounded by khurpis, spades, coir baskets, iron taslas and coils of thick rubber pipes, an old man with a drooping grey moustache, sat on a high takht behind a counter sporting a telephone on its dusty top.

'Ram Ram, Tauji,' he said to the shopkeeper whose glance was suddenly alert. 'Any idea where the murder took place?'

'Murder? Not in our village,' said the old man, miffed.

'Is this not Chandola village?' asked Adhirath.

The old man pointed to the sign at the railway station that sported the name of Jhandapur. 'You can't read?' he asked. 'Where are you from? What is your business here?'

'Ah, how did I miss that? So which way is Chandola? Any idea which farm?' Adhirath wished he had had his uniform on. That would have taught the old man some manners.

The taciturn shopkeeper pointed towards a road in front of the station. His moving finger dripped contempt on the strip of concrete that led to places where murders took place, bringing villages bad names and police jeeps.

Chandola was the next village down the road, a road that was narrow but surprisingly good and free from potholes of noticeable dimension. But as things turned out, he did not have to cross the village or seek directions. The farmhouse was a kilometre or so short of the untidy cluster of houses that went by the name of Chandola.

He could see a knot of gaping villagers at some distance down the road. Some had gamchas on their shoulders, some were in kurta pajama, some in shirt pants and some in banian pajamas. Some wore dhotis but most were in pajamas.

Killing the engine, he let the motorbike roll to the spot. The crowd was gazing at the gate from which a narrow lane led up to a rather pretty house, the kind he had seen in picture frames sold at the roadside bazaars that he had always wanted to buy and hang from the wall in his all-purpose room. There was a little rectangular depression in the wall, facing the bed, which looked custom-built for a scenery; but the frames were always either too small or too large.

And now he was looking at one such house. A large iron gate breached the thick sandstone walls of the farm. Two elephants, one on each wrought iron gate, held garlands of flowers in their trunks. They must face each other when the gate was closed, he thought, enviously eyeing the way the petals of every flower were detailed in the garland. This place dripped money. He wondered at the small size of the farm. He had always thought that farms were very large.

He pushed through the crowd towards the open gate. Just as he stepped onto the red carpet of the local sand—badarpur—leading inside, and laid a deliberately casual hand on the cold iron of the elephant's hind leg, two policemen came to the gate, a constable and an Assistant Sub Inspector, with a man from the village in an unwashed dhoti.

There was no jeep around so he guessed that Nitesh must

have left. Adhirath stood there silent, taking in the scene. Nitesh must have taken the body away to the morgue. On his way here he had seen no police jeep, or any handcart or bullock cart carting away a dead body. Perhaps there was another way out of the village or they went through Chandola, which lay ahead.

He felt a sudden stab of despair. Here he was, the day after a festival, come to catch up with his batch mate about old times, and his friend had been called away by the dead. By a dead stranger. His mother's voice played in his head: 'This is your situation in life; wherever you go, you only face death.'

He eased out of the crowd again, looking around to see if there was at least a chaiwala. No such luck. Only silent villagers. He tried a smile. Nobody smiled back. It was obvious that Nitesh had left behind an officer to record the statements of the villagers. A junior officer, the lowest in rank, but an officer all right, with a brass star on the shoulder of his uniform, just in case the villagers got offended that they had a murder case, no less, and yet the police found them deserving only of a constable. Nitesh had told him that handling such small ego problems is of prime significance in rural areas.

He heard the ASI tell the villager in the grubby dhoti, 'Tauji, you know, don't you, you know everything. I am only doing my duty. You will have to bring these boys to the thana to record the statement.'

'We will take a call on that. The boys have already told you what they had to. We don't want thana kachahari,' said another sulky old man in pajamas.

'What have we done? We have already told you what we saw. Is that a crime?' asked a young man in a soiled white shirt and pajama bottoms, the strings of which hung out. 'We can't do this thana kachahari.'

'Pradhanji, you know that paperwork has to be done. You have so many registers to fill in your panchayat, don't you?' This man could be the murderer himself and yet a police officer was pleading with him, thought Adhirath. Well, that is how things work; the man who first sees the dead body is always the first suspect even though later he may turn out to be a completely innocent bystander.

A woman tore through the crowd to reach the ASI.

'You talk to me, I am a member of the Panchayat. I have won the elections here,' she said.

'Arre, am I not handling it? Let me handle this,' said the man in the dhoti. He seemed annoyed by her interference.

'Sarpanchji, you are now an ex-sarpanch, that is why these people are not listening to you,' the woman did not seem the type to be easily silenced. 'Listen, it is like this that in our village nobody has ever gone to a police station. Just understand this. Murder has been done, in a faramhouse. No villager ever comes here. We have never set foot in the faramhouse till now. These people will come and spread filth in the village and we will go to the thana? Whoever heard such rubbish? Where does this rule come from?'

The man in the dhoti got truly angry at this. 'What business do you have here? Better you go home and cook. Why are you putting your feet into men's business? Have I forgotten how to behave like a sarpanch, only because I am now an ex-sarpanch? I can still fill the details of all forty registers of the panchayat with closed eyes. Better you not talk about filth being spread in the village; have you seen any filth?'

Voices were being raised. Standing alone on the fringes of the crowd, Adhirath began to feel lonely. Nitesh should not have scooted like this, leaving his subordinates to handle such touchy villagers. After all, does the in-charge of the case have some accountability or not?

The ASI raised both his hands and begged for peace. 'We all know that Pradhanji called the police. We have to record that. He has also signed on the panchnama...I only request that you just give me a statement that you saw the dead body...'

'We did not see the body,' said the former sarpanch. 'We heard, and we told what we heard.'

The pradhan standing next to him uttered a loud 'haan' in agreement and stared at the ASI. Then turning to the current woman panch, he said, 'Now you see what happens when you interfere? You will truly drag the village into the dust. I had told you, we don't need you here, there is no need for you to come here.'

'Won't people ask me what were you doing when such a big kaand happened in the village? They have voted for me so they will definitely ask,' the woman panch protested loudly. 'Listen Inspector, nobody from our village is involved, so why will they go to the police station? Just see what will happen to if you dare touch anyone from the village, I dare you.'

Some boys laughed. One of them said, 'So Chachi, will you grab his hair and push him out of the village?'

'Actually, Chachi was right when she said we should not call the police, those people who own the faram, it is their headache, let them deal with it,' someone said loudly.

'She has fought elections, she knows everything,' another voice added.

Adhirath recognized the usual confrontation between the police and the people—the people refusing to part with information and the police refusing to budge. Except, this ASI was actually being nice—he was whining, he was pleading, his head was bowed a little. He was not threatening to tie them all up and drag them to the thana. Perhaps this was because he knew that the village was one entity you did not touch here. Even in cases of murder. Adhirath had heard of such things, this was the first time he was watching it manifest itself.

The ASI mounted his motorcycle. The crowd parted and within seconds, vanished as though it had been swallowed up by the earth. One second they were all there, in kurtas and banians, pants and pajamas, and the moment the policemen rode away, they had all melted away into the fields. The only players left were the pradhan addressed earlier as tauji, the former sarpanch and three young men who had presumably found the dead woman.

'Ka ho Pradhanji, jaanaa padega?' one of them asked.

'Why would you have to go? They need the statement, let them come here, the dogs,' Pradhanji's anger showed no signs of abating. 'Is it not enough that bitches choose to be killed in our blameless village? Are we to now do thana kachahari also for them?'

Adhirath lit a cigarette, instantly attracting attention. 'Hey, are you one of the police? A jasoos?' asked one of the young men in a striped pajama and blue shirt.

Adhirath decided on a judicious untruth. 'Actually I was passing by and I saw this,' he said gesturing at the gate, 'and stopped. Just like that.' Then presenting the pack of cigarettes to the old men he said, 'Ram Ram, Tauji.'

Nobody took the proffered cigarette. The men continued to glare at him. Adhirath shrugged and went back to his mobike and to prove that his intention was not suspect and he was only a passer-by, he kick started it and sped away in the direction ahead of Chandola village. In the middle of the village, he had to skirt three potholes, one, particularly large and filled with dirty water. But the moment he crossed the village he once again saw the gleaming road, leading into nowhere. It looked as if the straight and flat road had been lying there waiting for a vehicle to tread it. Who can refuse such an invitation? He rode on, tracing the gentle curves the road took for nearly three kilometres. Not a shop. No tea vendor. Not even a cigarette and paan kiosk. He knew he should have gone back towards Jhandapur. At least there was a little market there. It was close to the station and he would have found some tea and a bite to eat.

But the attraction of the silent fields would not let go. He stopped the motorcycle, leaned it against a tree and walked to the shade of another tree. Fields on both sides. Mustard ripening in the sun. Nitesh must be in the morgue by now. He would not be able to meet him now. In some farms he could see small beds of vegetables, with gaps in between where some of the vegetables had been pulled out. He looked around. He wished there was someone he could ask for a radish. So late in the season he could not tell which would be tender enough to eat and which were past the eat-by date. If only someone would come this way and give him a radish. Or a carrot, juicy and red, from the earth. How nice would it be to rub the soil from the vegetables, polish them with some leaves; who knows the villager might even have given him some water with which to wash them. It would be so refreshing to eat such fresh vegetables still smelling of the soil. He was tempted to lie down in the shade of the tree and take a nap.

Adhirath looked around. A crow pecked at something on a dung heap close by, from which stuck out empty packets of chips, blue and red and yellow and many bags of thin polythene. It was so quiet that he felt guilty when he started his bike. But he had to return. He started back, determined that if he saw those villagers again he would belch some smoke in their faces. He saw no one as he passed the farmhouse, even though he slowed down. Then, out of the corner of his eye, he caught a glimpse of a woman sitting alone against the wall of the farmhouse.

He drove past but something pulled him back. He could not say what it was—a build-up of restless energy from so many days of doing nothing? The lurking response of a cop to a crime? A regret for not having beaten back the unnecessary aggression of those young raw men, uncouth in their pajamas? A simmering discontent at not having taken up the challenge those anarchic villagers had thrown at him?—but he slowed down, stopped and walked the bike towards the gate, his helmet still slung from the side. The garlands in the trunks of elephants were now facing each other.

She was an old woman, a small woman, and she was sobbing quietly. Her hair was grey and unkempt, in the loose plait that was rolled into a bun hung on the back of her neck. Her faded blue sari was a nylon, a mismatched black blouse hung over her pendulous breasts. On her feet were old chappals worn at the heels. Whether the aanchal of her sari refused to stay put on her breasts or had simply slid off from there because of the way she was shivering as she tried to hold back her sobs was not clear.

That is what must have caught my attention, he thought. Unlike women of her class, she was not beating her breasts or howling loudly. She wept quietly and almost shrank into the wall, hiding, as if afraid to attract attention. One end of her pallu was stuffed in her mouth in an attempt to stifle the sobs that broke through the wad of cloth.

He squatted next to her.

'Why are you crying, amma?' he asked gently.

She did not spring up in surprise or retreat. Whether she had heard him was also doubtful. She simply raised her eyes to his and the dumb agony in them was wild with complaints against an unjust cosmos.

She spoke after a long while.

'She was my daughter,' she said. 'She was. What a horrible death she died.'

'That girl? Inside there? Tell me.'

Now the old woman looked alarmed.

'I am not from the village. You know that, don't you? Here, let us go to the market. We will get some tea,' he said.

She slunk back and got up to leave.

'Amma, okay, forget the tea. Let us sit here. Let us. Tell me. I may be able to help.'

She did not seem to trust him. He could see that trust had been the first of the treasures the old woman had lost in her life. Her wary eyes, her silent sobs, her shrunken frame, everything a testimony to the loss of faith in life and people. Her sobs were no longer wet. They were dry and crackled like fire. Her eyes were now alert.

He said, 'Amma, these villagers, they will not give statement to police. They won't tell the police anything. I heard them say that. They hated her.'

'She was not a good girl,' said the old woman.

'That I don't know. But see, what god has given man must not take. God gave her life and we don't know who took it. Tell me what happened. I am like your son,' he said. 'Did you see how she was killed?'

She gasped then and stared at him with wide eyes as if she could not see him at all. He had no idea how she was killed. He could call Nitesh and ask. But his statement had shaken the old woman.

'Even animals are not slaughtered like that. They don't cut even goats like that.' She began to wail loudly then. He was afraid the hostile villagers would come back. A bunch of children had stopped in a field some distance away and were staring at them.

'Amma, these villagers will come back. Let us walk towards the station,' he said and leading his motorbike, motioned to her to walk with him. She stuffed her pallu into her mouth again and walked with him. After a while she agreed to ride pillion and he brought her to the railway station.

There was no tea to be found at the station. He bought two bottles of Coca-Cola and a packet of biscuits from a shop in the market close by and forced a cola on the woman. Sitting next to her on the bench, he sighed. He should now get up and leave. He had stopped to console and was being drawn in by the woman's obvious reluctance to talk. He decided not to press her any more.

But perversely, she began on her own, after a few sips from the bottle. She talked slowly, and between sobs told him about her ill-fated daughter. That is how Adhirath got to know that the girl who had been killed had a name and a dream too. Ramwati, now sipping cola next to him, had named her daughter Suryabala for her shining face. Adhirath wondered whether the name had turned into a curse, leaving her dead in the blazing sunlight.

Suryabala was her youngest daughter, the naughty girl who had studied up to class four, the girl who pinched choice pieces of meat from the plates of her three elder brothers. She always wanted the best of everything—clothes, hairclips, food. How much can you get in a dhobi's house? There was little work and less money. Who gives clothes to dhobis to wash nowadays? Amirpur is not a place where you can score laundry contracts for hotels. You have to depend on farm work. By the time Suryabala was sixteen Ramwati married her off.

'The ill-fated girl was very pretty,' Ramwati said. 'The whole world knows that if you have a face like the moon then your fate will be like a sieve. Pleasure will never last. She was married to a fellow in Delhi. In Manglapuri. There too she would roam around the bazaars, eating chaat or chattering with anyone and everyone. Scoldings, beatings, kicks, nothing kept her in control. She was an ill omen, that girl. Her father died when she was only two. She brought bad luck to the family.'

Ramwati broke down and cried long and loud. Adhirath sat unmoved. He did not even feel like consoling her now. He had left home looking for some happiness and he had found this instead. He began to regret getting involved. This was Nitesh's headache, why should he get mixed up in this affair. He must go home now.

Ramwati wiped her tears, blew her nose in her pallu and continued her tale of woe. Who could tell how unlucky her daughter was, not even the jyotishi who had cast her horoscope when she was less than a week old. She took her father and then she was widowed. After only two years of marriage. Her in-laws would not feed her properly. How could Ramwati blame them? After all Suryabala had not even given them a son to carry on their name.

'She came back to us. But she was no grieving widow, I tell you. She had developed airs by living in the city. She would wear coloured bangles and bright saris. Which decent woman does this? And which man will leave such a woman alone? They say that men of the same village are like your brothers or uncles but that is only a myth. Her sisters-in-law also found a good excuse now to keep bickering. We thought if she is so fond of bright colours and jewellery, she should be married again. Heaven knows she was pretty. Not a blemish on that full-moon face. We found a nice man and got her married off again.

'Do you know what she did, that horrible girl? She ran away in a fortnight, can you believe it? The first time her brothers thrashed her and sent her back. But she kept coming back to us. Three times we made her go back. Kept her locked up in a room. Thrashed her with sticks. The fourth time, she refused to go. Said his mouth smells like a rotten fish. Said her brother-in-law had designs on her. That her husband rode her all night, would not let her rest at all. The last time she came back to us we folded our hands in front of her in-laws and asked them to grant her a divorce. The biradari panchayat arranged the divorce and fined us. They were asking for ten thousand rupees. Somehow we got them to agree on six thousand. We had to feed the whole panchayat, all fifty-three men. Only then they gave her permission for a separation.

'Her brothers said they would not keep her. But where would she go? I wish I had throttled her in the cradle. She wanted to learn the work in a booty parlour; that is what she said. She did learn too. Then she found a job in one of those parlours. Yes, she took the train from here to go to town and came back and people said all kinds of horrid things. Sometimes she did not even come home at night. Village louts hung at the station platform or outside, waiting for her and passing lewd comments. They offered her money. We could hardly show our faces in public. It is good that we are not from this village. Once, the pardhan of Chandola sent a man to our house. He brought the message that if the girl wants to do business, men in the village have lots of money. Just send the girl to the toobwell tomorrow,' she said and fell silent.

'Tubewell?' asked Adhirath.

'In the fields they have toobwells...'

'Yes, I know tubewells.'

'...they have a room there. For the electricity plugs and meters. That is where they do all their dirty business,' said the old woman. 'That day her brothers finally threw her out. Who knows where she went? She came to meet me twice. Sporting a big tikuli on her forehead, this big a bindi. Anklets and earrings tinkled on her. No bangles now, now she wore big kangans. Sisters-in-law made a face when they saw her.

'She definitely met the fate she deserved. She died the way she lived, filthy. But she was my daughter. I gave birth to her, she came out of here,' said the old woman pointing to her abdomen. Her tears had dried up now. 'Someone will have to perform her last rites. Where have they taken her body? Those bastard policemen, may God roast them in hell, never told me anything. They did not even tell me where they have taken her, how will I get her body? My poor daughter...' she broke down again.

'The police who told you about her death?' said Adhirath. 'They took away the body.'

'Police? What police? A man from the village came, sent by the pardhan. He told me. He said your daughter has been cut open, her intestines are lying in the mud. I ran here. The way I was. By the time I got here they had taken her away. The police did not even come to find me, talk to me.'

'Ammaji, come I will drop you home. I will find out who did this. I will tell you,' he said and could not believe that the words were his. His voice sounded like that of a stranger's, as if someone was standing outside him and making this assurance to the old woman and he did not like it at all.

He led her down the stairs of the station and took her back to her village on his motorcycle. That is how he first visited Amirpur and saw her little house—a pile of bricks behind a walled-in courtyard with an asbestos sheet as roof.

2

Adhirath told himself that the assurance he had given Ramwati was like the ritual consolation offered to the bereaved, offered with the intention of keeping them as weak as their expectations would have been. He had not been able to talk to Nitesh either. However, the next day, his restlessness began to grow so he left the house again heading straight to the nearest English Wine and Beer shop.

Peeling away from the crowd outside the booze shop he tucked the addha, the half bottle, under his shirt. As he strode back to the mobike he noticed a crane clutching a car in its jaws, towing it away and bumping it around. The little car looked forlorn as it followed the crane, its bowed forehead licking the ground. A man in a suit was berating a fruitwala who had set up his mobile street shop right in front of the line of untidily parked cars. As the fruit seller moved away, the man cranked open the door of a car and aimed a kick at Adhirath's motorbike parked right across his headlights. Just aimed, he did not kick it. Adhirath had by then arrived and calmly opening the little storage box by the side of the seat, he began packing in the booze bottle.

'Is this your bike?' Mr Suit asked in an infuriated tone.

'No. I stole it,' said Adhirath to him arrogantly as he clicked shut the locker cabinet. Then climbing on, he said 'Jaa police bula le,' and laughed uproariously as he sped away while English epithets pursued him futilely, drowning in the loud roar of his bike. After all it was an Enfield. The Hondas of today may flaunt their wide fibreglass breasts but they were no match to the old sinner of an Enfield.

He arrived at the mortuary soon after lunch. The morgue was behind the thick walls of the old building and he knew it well. He had been to this low-ceilinged garage-like place several times. He went round to the entrance of the morgue and stopped at the open doors. Entry was restricted but the guard knew him and sometimes let him in. Sometimes the guard dozed off after lunch so he quickly slipped in. Today the guard raised a hand to forbid him from entering and looked too alert for him to try his tricks. Adhir thought that his ill fate was still accompanying him. Perhaps a VIP had died. That means there were doctors inside. He began to chat with the guard. Spotting a staff member passing by, Adhir asked him to tell Bhikulal that he was waiting outside. The guard laughed and added that he was a real VIP for Bhikulal.

Bhikulal emerged after half an hour.

'You keep your son-in-law waiting do you? Tauba, tauba how much the world has changed!' said Adhirath.

'Arre all those sasuras are inside. I can't leave a postmortem in the middle,' he said.

'Yes, I guessed it the moment I arrived. I thought now that the Ganga is flowing in reverse, nobody sends a packet of sweets on Holi, sons-in-law are waiting on their fathers-in-law, I might as well bring you a gift.' He fished out the bottle.

Bhiku took it but did not look happy. 'You could have got me a full bottle for a change considering how I never charged you anything for the work I did for you, being as you are the son-in-law. Not easy I tell you, I am not the only one who takes his fees. Everybody does. It is not a small thing. The money does not go into my pocket alone. Everybody demands fees. You will die if I told you what the surgeon charges. And I am the best in this business. There is no doubt about it. Nobody is better at postmortem than I am.'

A half a bottle of rum was his fees for any postmortem and business had been truly good in the last two years. At least one body arrived every day, on good days as many as three people got murdered, that is the three who get to the newspapers. The others nobody even counted.

They chatted for a while as Bhiku asked after his niece and reduced two beedis to foul ash.

'What is happening with the enquiry?' asked Bhiku.

'Will happen in its time.'

'Had you accepted my gift of a jageer, you would have had something to do today. Everything does not have to be done personally, you can employ people to do it for you. You would have got some share at least.'

Bhikulal had offered a residential territory to Adhirath as dowry where his family had the exclusive traditional contract for cleaning the area. Sweeping staircases, taking out garbage. A nice source of income but an embarrassed Adhirath and his family had refused, despite many pleadings.

After a while Adhirath came to the point.

'Mamu, did you cut up that girl who was killed in the farmhouse?'

'The one who was brought here on Tuesday? I did, only yesterday. There was a long queue. Why? You know her?'

'Just curious. My friend is looking into the case,' he said. 'In charge.'

'I know. He came here and was trying to rob me of my addha. Tell me who can work in this stinking place without something to stiffen the nerves? You need liquor in your bones to work here, pure liquor. Those doctors, they have blood in their veins so they can't even come inside the morgue. If they did, they would die of the smell alone. They spend crores on education. These sasuras, they get degrees to loot patients. It is a business. When I joined here, there used to be more bahman doctors; now there are banias. That alone is enough to tell you what a good business this doctory is. Now, I don't have a degree but I can teach them a few things. I am the first to get to know how the people died. Died of fetty leever or kidney cracked open or intestines bloated like balloons, died naturally or killed? You know about the bomb blast case, don't you? How many bodies were brought here! In many, many pieces. It wasn't clear which arm belonged to whom. Which stomach had which arms. Who do you think pieced together bodies from scattered parts? I did,' said Bhiku as he smote himself on the chest with pride.

Adhir sat on his bike, twirling the keyring on his index finger. He had heard this before. He suppressed a yawn. 'Those white coats, who go to nice classrooms and sit on benches—they did not even come here to see what people blown up by bombs look like. I tell you, they look like pieces of watermelon. You have seen seeds in watermelon? Exactly like them there were black spots in the bodies. You know what they were? Intestines. Stuff inside the intestines. There is all that they had eaten a while ago—samosa, pakoda, roti, korma...'

Adhirath yawned again. He had the heard the short version of this human jigsaw story, the long version and the longest one too. Bhiku enjoyed telling him how intestines are several kilometres long and are so nicely coiled and packed inside the abdomen. 'That grey rope, that is your large intestine. Several kilometres of it packed inside that much area. All coiled up and full of shit. Black and yellow.'

The first time Adhir had heard the story he had puked many times and had not been able to eat anything and screamed at Pushpa, 'I will never meet your Mamaji again.'

But he came again and again to meet this man, the bhangi at the morgue who had not been able to expel the victims of a bomb blast from his stomach. He was still at it: 'It was I who pieced them together, only then the doctors prepared their reports.'

'Mamu, that girl, the body that came from the farmhouse...'

'I told your friend—no addha no postmortem, no report. He began to tell me that he is my son-in-law's friend. That is all right, I told him, but you are not the lover of this girl, are you? If you are, you will have to pay double fees. Doctors will write report only after I give them leever-sapleen-this-that in jars. They only peer into the microscope. Give me a microscope. I bet I will learn in six months. There is nobody better at postmortem than me. I told him clearly: No addha, no postmortem...'

'Okay, okay, I will get you his addha too,' said Adhirath, trying to cut this short.

'I got it out of him all right. Two addhas instead of one,' said Bhiku.

'I want the report,' said Adhirath.

'Report will come only after a week. Only after all these motherfucking white coats have done everything they can to put off work. Only the likes of us work. Look, we cut up bodies and everyone hates us. We are untouchables. They also don't touch us, motherfuckers. Chattering away in English all the time. You know there is not a single student here from my caste? Not one. All these bloody bahmans and banias come here to the morgue to cut up dead bodies to learn what a man is made of inside and do you think that knowledge ever makes them see all of us as human? No way, my son, no way. Most of those bodies are of people like us. Us people, poor sisterfuckers, lawaaris. And you know what? These bloody vegetarians who once thought the dead body was untouchable and will still have sutak when someone in the family dies, these people come and eat rasgullas at the morgue sometimes. I swear they do. They will do anything for money, these upper castes. I will let you in on a secret. Nowadays more banias are becoming doctors. Good business it is. Private hospitals. Pharma company bounties. Rich people paying lakhs to get their hearts cut and stitched. Banias are becoming doctors and dipping their hands in blood. Come to think of it, they always had their hands in people's blood.'

'Yes, yes, but can you tell me the cause of death?'

'They say he was being harassed in the college hostel by all these upper caste doctor students. They made him wash their clothes and flung chapattis at him in the mess and said he must not touch the bowl of vegetables or it would be polluted. He committed suicide. Such a hulla bulla. The media is here and you will see three days later nobody will talk of him and nothing will change. Coward, bloody coward. That is what he was. Did not even think what his mother will feel, how his sister will live. Just hanged himself. He should have flung the bowls in their faces. Or killed some of them. Arre, he had decided to die, so why not kill a few first? Instead, he kills himself. Quitters all.'

Adhirath sighed. The problem with this man was that he was part of a union and loved making speeches. He had become such a nuisance for the authorities that just to be rid of him they had posted him at the morgue. Punishment posting. Sweepers paid huge bribes to be allowed to avoid this duty. This one revelled in it. He hardly had the time for the union now or even any interest in it for he rinsed his mouth with rum when he got up in the morning. He arrived drunk and he left drunk. How he managed to cut up bodies so accurately, Adhirath had never understood.

'Mamu, the body my friend got?' said Adhirath.

'Who? Oh, that girl who was brought in today? No, no, Tuesday. Yes Tuesday it was, or was it Wednesday?'

'I am talking about the girl who was killed in the farmhouse,' said Adhirath, clearly demonstrating impatience through the patient enunciation of each word.

'Oh, that's your friend's case? That is why you are here? How is the enquiry going?'

'What enquiry?'

'Your case. How is it going? You pay attention to your case and stop meddling in other people's business. Your friend is police. He will get report. Tell me have they filed report in your case?'

'They will file the report when they have the time. I am not their first priority. And if you don't want to talk to me you just have to say it. I am leaving,' said Adhirath with some asperity.

'I hope it is soon. After all you were innocent and they must reinstate you,' said Bhiku.

'Mamu, the girl. How did she die?'

Bhiku looked at him with sad eyes.

'My niece never asks this favour but you are a different variety altogether. I say nobody must have a policeman in the family and I have two. Obviously there will be no peace for me.'

'Mamu, I came to you with great hopes.'

'That girl was strangled. Marks on the throat, just below the chin. But I don't think she died of that. She had a long gash in her abdomen. A very long one. Very precise and straight, like someone held a ruler and cut her against its edge. How they managed to cut like that I have no idea. Bastard must have been quite a practiced cutter, whoever did it. Just made my job easy even though the body was a mess. They had stuffed the intestines somehow inside, all the mud sticking to it...'

Adhirath began to make motions of getting on to his bike. Bhiku lit another beedi. They both sat staring at the harried faces of patients and relatives braving the traffic fumes, marching to the tune of honking horns.

'Can't imagine how he cut her in so straight a line. He must have got injured. It is possible that there is something under her nails, a little skin or blood of the cutter. The girl also had many wounds. Looks like someone had beaten her up. Lips too, someone had bitten the lips perhaps, they were swollen. Many bruises on her chest. And look some bruises between her thighs also, on her thighs I mean. The palms also have a bruise like she was dragged and was trying to resist. Must have all happened before she was strangled.

'How was she strangled? Hands?'

'Na. Rope. You could see the rope stains on her throat. Thick rope it must have been. You can see the weave on the skin.

He paused, sighed. 'Girl was pregnant also. Three months or so. The baby was also cut into two pieces. Pheetus, they call it. Just a blob of flesh you know. Looks like a fish standing upright. I am telling the truth. It does not have features. Have you seen anything like that? They keep them in jars, in saline solution. Want me to show you? Well this pheetus, it was cut into two, neat. The intestines too were criss-crossed with cuts. You know why? They are coiled up inside and when you wield a knife on a coil it cuts many parts of the coil. Try it on a coil of rope. Did they teach you that in the police teeraining school? How to cut up dolls so you can see what kind of cut what kind of knife makes? You can do it today, stuff a some rope inside a doll, then cut the doll with a knife and look at the coil and see.'

Adhirath had heard enough. He got up and walked a few steps. Then he turned back and said, 'Let us have tea.'

Bhiku spat a laugh at him. 'Throw up behind that pillar. There under that window. What kind of a man are you? And a policeman at that? My niece, what she saw in you, I have no idea. You know she was never afraid of anything. Not even ghosts. Never.'

Bending over behind a pillar, Adhirath heard none of this.

'Mamu, you are saying she died of that cut?' he asked afterwards.

'Yes. Or both. First she lost some of her breath and could not run, then she lost a lot of blood. Poor girl. She was a very pretty girl. And young too. Quite young. A little older than my niece. Does she have any other children?'

Adhirath shook his head and left. It was late afternoon by the time he got home. Pushpa was in the kitchen making tea. His father's voice was raging like the fire.

'In my young age, we used to have real tea. Milk was boiled for so long it used to turn pink. I swear it used to. Pink. Woman would be sitting near the chulha, cutting vegetables and the milk would be on simmer on a very low flame. The tea was so thick a spoon wouldn't sink if you put it on top. Cream would float on the surface...'

Mother wasn't around, must have gone to the market.

'Want me to chop vegetables?' Adhirath asked, standing close behind Pushpa. Pushpa turned to look at him. Her eyebrows were raised. Her eyes laughed into his.

When Adhirath finally met Nitesh in the thana, the conversation had to begin with the talk about the enquiry against him. Most times, Adhir had to put on a martyr face. Not with Nitesh. Nitesh got him the gossip from the department.

'No idea when it will be done, no clue,' said Nitesh.

'Yaar, it would be good if it were finished early. If they want to dismiss me, let them do it. Staying at home like this, my life is ruined. Nothing to do man, I just can't bear it anymore.'

'Lucky you,' said Nitesh, 'you can sleep as much as you want. No work, nobody to answer to and still on half salary. Nobody is going to ask you why burglaries have gone up. Or when a murder will be solved. Look at me, I have been lying here in this rotten room. Can't even step outside. Mosquitoes give you no respite. On top of that, it was a full moon night. You can't even switch off the moon.'

'What is the story of that murder?'

'What story? She was a whore, that bitch. That very day she was identified. Everybody in the village knew her. Used to work in some beauty parlour. In this very market. You know what goes on behind the curtains there. Massages, massages of all sorts, kela massage. Looks like there was more than one man, must have held her tight, that is how they managed to slit her open in such a straight line. Must have had a lot of practice in cutting. From here to here,' said Nitesh running a finger from his chest to the thighs in a sharp straight line.

Adhirath shivered.

'On the day of Holi too,' said Nitesh with his brows raised. 'Played Holi with blood. Had she been sitting at home like a decent woman, had she had a job in some office she would be playing with her kids now. This is the consequence of playing parlour-parlour.'

Adhir looked at Nitesh carefully. They had met at training college. They had got drunk together, sung romantic film songs heard in their teens, tunelessly but together. They had been mad about Neetu Singh. They recited Sahir's '*Kabhi kabhi mere dil me khayal aataa hai...*' struggling to get the Urdu pronunciation right. Now he could not find a single sign of those days in the lineaments of his friend. What had happened to the poetry? Nitesh's solid body seemed completely resistant to poetry. Now it was fuck this one's mother and that one's sister. Does a thana make you like this? Are gaalis stored in the maalkhana? Do they first get one, once in a while, and then become part of your armoury and then part of your personality? Perhaps the year-long suspension from the job had pulled those words out of him; that and Pushpa's daily admonitions not to abuse in front of their son and to ask his father not to use gaalis before the child either. He had had to place his hand on the child's head and swear that he would not use cuss words at home, but Bapu was made of sterner stuff. For many years, Pushpa had insisted on living away from his family; she found it difficult to live with the constant abuse there. They rang out in the house and in the lane too. The tent people verbally raped the mothers and sisters of everyone they talked about all day long. At home his dad would fill in the gaps. But then Pushpa too had actually become a little tough to live with ever since she got posted to the women's helpline, Adhirath thought. The first time he had met her in the thana, this hawaldarni had not been like this.

'Even a whore should not be killed. Was the murder related to her profession? What happened? She went thinking there will be two clients and there were four, she refused? Or they asked her to do something she would not?'

'Ask a jyotish, he will tell you. How would I know? I don't

know what kind of people go to such women. On top of that, these villagers! Man, I tell you those villagers we used to see in Bombay films, remember those characters? Simple, innocent souls who always spoke the truth? You won't find a single such person in the village. Saale, they have all fallen silent as if someone has taped their mouths. Nobody has seen anything. The guard, he is a bastard of his own kind. That day we could not find him. Went again in the evening and then we found him. That too we got the information with great difficulty from someone. We dragged him here, gave two tight slaps too, you know...he is an outsider. Even if you kill him, no villager will come here to protest. Now this fellow, he locks the gate and opens it for everyone. Says nobody came there. In fact, he says he was not there at all. Says he went to play Holi. Tell me, he must have gone only in the day. Where was he at night? Says he was high on bhang and passed out in the room of some other guard at some other farmhouse two kilometres away.'

'So who found the dead body?'

'Three louts. They say they never go to the farm. Sometimes they go to get mulberry but even that the guard gives them so there is no need to go in. That day the guard wasn't to be seen so they went in. The body was under the mulberry trees. So they ran to the pradhan. He called us.'

'Strange, na? The villagers would hardly let an outsider play Holi with them,' said Adhirath. 'So where did he go?'

'Who knows? Possible that the villagers did let him play for a while and then he went off to another farmhouse. There are just farmhouses on both sides of the road there. Wonder where the fields of the villages are.'

'Must have been sold.'

'No, there are some fields. Some of the villagers do sharecropping in the farmhouses also.'

'Oh, well, then you won't be able to leave the thana. I had thought we could go watch *Munnabhai MBBS*.'

'Yaar, I have heard that it is a great fun film. But the day we join this job we have to divorce the rest of life. Talak, talak, talak,' said Nitesh. Both laughed loud.

'What do you think, was it a planned murder?'

'Am finding out. Do you know what is interesting? In the village everyone says, "Ladki dekh raakhi hai. Lekin parlour ka naam-vaam na jaante." Saw the girl but did not know the name of the parlour. Of course, they wouldn't know the parlour's name. Even her mother did not know. In this little market, do you know how many parlours there are? Seventeen! Seems as if nowadays women get themselves done up before they go to even buy vegetables. We went round asking everyone, showed her picture to people. Then we discovered that she did indeed work for a parlour; yaar look, here, so close to our thana, in a parlour called Kiliopetra. I asked: what kind of name is this? Got to know she was some queen of Egypt, very beautiful. And she used to plaster her face with our gwarpatha. These people call it aloe vera. So now that thing has a big market. Take eight annas worth of gwarpatha, churn it in a mixer, slap it on the face and charge hundred rupees for it. I am thinking of getting the missus to run a parlour. Another interesting thing, here she had told people her name was Renu. And her mother told us some other name. Now tell me, if she had to just have a job in a parlour, why would she change her name? The actual business must have been something else. Parlour people say they know nothing. That day the parlour was closed anyways. They said her work was okay. She was pretty so she also got many clients. She had been taught to say that the parlour uses local products. Women, I tell you, so easy to fool them. I have to go out now.

Have to go meet the owner of that farm. In Preet Vihar. Will you come? Your house is on the way, I can drop you there.'

'I'll come with you,' Adhir said.

'You're very interested in this case? Kya chakkar hai?'

Adhir smiled and said, 'What is there for me to do at home, why should I go so early? I am bored, yaar. My skills will rust away. I will come with you. If I get reinstated, I might end up like a newbie.'

'And here I thought you were coming to help me,' Nitesh complained mockingly.

'Why do you need help? You alone are enough to crack the case,' Adhir said.

The last one year had stolen some of his arrogance and had given him enough cleverness to accept the truth that however close a relationship, a little bit of flattery keeps irritants away. It is good to talk about honesty but never good to practice it.

'Some people are very lucky,' Nitesh was saying. 'This village girl. Who would have bothered about her death? But look, the saali went and got murdered in a farmhouse. Now she is making headlines.'

Adhirath nodded in agreement. Soon Nitesh would also be in the newspapers if he arrested the murder accused.

'I am not in uniform,' he said.

'Let them think that a plainclothesman has come along, someone from CID. As if they know about police procedure. This much knowledge only seasoned goons have.'

'They have more knowledge than us,' said Adhirath bitterly.

'That is true. You are paying the price for it,' said Nitesh and slapped a morose-looking Adhir's back. 'Yaar that mama of bhabhi is very interesting. This is the first time I had to deal with him. Got two addhas from me. One for postmortem, the other for being the friend of his son-in-law!'

Both laughed uproariously.

When the jeep arrived at J.J. Bindal's Preet Vihar house, nobody asked the Inspector who was with him.

Adhirath had never understood why the dome that looked so grand in Humayun's Tomb began to look like an onion the moment its size went down. The onion was the tallest thing in this building. There were two bow-shaped terraces on either side which formed the roofing of the rest of the house. This is what he was contemplating while sitting under the onion that the crorepati had installed on his house. Nitesh was staring at the roof, which was of such a dark blue hue it looked black. Light glimmered from scattered holes in the ceiling.

'Yaar, I have seen such a ceiling in the planetarium,' he said to Adhir.

Adhir laughed. They had been waiting for ten minutes. No sign of Bindal, not even one of his servants. This is how the rich show minor officials their place.

'Sorry, sorry, I was having a little bath,' said a thin man, entering the room. He looked annoyed.

Adhir studied him carefully. A raw silk kurta, pajamas with wide bottoms. He wasn't yet bald. Had he had a proper bath or just a little one? He shook his head forcefully. Bindal was cribbing that nobody had even served 'tea shea' to the guests. Two servants appeared with tea and snacks.

'Is that your farmhouse?' Nitesh asked him after some preliminaries.

'Yes, it is ours.'

'Did you know that girl, that woman whose body was found there?'

Bindal did not answer immediately. Adhir saw that the old man was very clever. He was trying to figure out how much truth to tell and how many lies he could get away with.

'I had seen her...came here a couple of times. Parduman got her. Our driver. We did not talk. She was some relative of his, some distant cousin.'

Nitesh found out that Parduman was on duty the day of Holi and was here. According to Bindal there was no question of his going to the farm despite the fact that he did everything that needed doing there. He seemed forthright. It did not appear as if he was hiding anything. Perhaps the annoyance he had displayed in the beginning was because he did not like the police coming to his house. Adhirath had never liked this aspect of his job. Nobody ever appeared pleased to see the police. He enjoyed watching people cringe but he also knew that the moment their backs were turned people hurled the filthiest of abuses at them. He was certain that till now he had only gathered the curses of people. People like Bindal, who are known as 'big people' in common parlance, cannot function without having the police in their pockets. That is why they must hate them even more since they had been pressured to buy what they did not want to buy. But then they know how to talk to the police without being scared.

'Where were you on the day of Holi?' Nitesh asked.

'Here. Where would we go? My astrologer had asked me to stay away from red colour. So you know, I never got out of the house. Got even the red curtains of the house changed and yet what should not have happened did happen. Everything is in the stars,' Bindal looked at the glittering stars on the ceiling of his house and spread his hands in a gesture of helplessness.

'Any witnesses?'

'You are suspecting me?' For the first time Bindal's eyebrows were raised in a frown. It seemed as if he would now say, 'You don't know me; the police commissioner is my locker room buddy.'

'It is our job. You keep answering questions,' said Nitesh picking up two slim slivers of Kaju katli that had been served with tea.

Bindal told them that in the day there had been a Holi party at home. There were two pots of bhang. Bhang pakoras had also been made. There was a lot going on. Everyone had been told not to get red gulaal but whoever listens? They had said: '*You* may have to avoid it, why should we bother?'

'How many people came to the party?' Nitesh did not like it that he had finished his statement so fast. He had just started on the gujhiya. What top quality sweets were these! Definitely not from the neighbourhood Aggrawal Sweets. These were even more delicious than the ones at Nathu's. Must have got them made by some special halwai.

'Must have been around fifty,' Bindal replied promptly.

Nitesh's heart sank. Now he would have to interview so many to discover who went missing for how long and when.

'How long did the party go on?' Adhirath asked his first question. He began to feel that his skills were truly fading. He had not even asked what time the woman had been killed. Perhaps Nitesh knew.

'Who can remember?' This time Bindal looked at Adhir carefully. 'People were high on bhang. They just lay here and there. Holi parties are like that only. More tea?' he yelled for the servant.

They talked for over an hour. They found out that four people lived in the house: Bindal, his eldest son and daughter-in-law, and a ten-year-old grandson. The younger son had moved to Kota in Rajasthan and had just begun a new business of gold jewellery. The second son used to live in this very house till last year but had started obsessing about opening a hotel in the hills and began demanding his share of the wealth.

'Who ever transfers property to the name of sons while alive? I had invested some money in the business for him when he was born, we do that whenever a child is born. I asked the munshi to calculate how much it had grown to, and I gave him half. It was quite substantial. Both daughters are settled. They too live in Delhi. Not a big family. The mother of my children died two years back. After that the family is sort of breaking up, scattering,' Bindal told them the whole story of the family. His mocking tone had vanished.

'Even then fifty people came to the party. Who were they?' asked Nitesh.

'Some business contacts. Most were relatives. Whoever meets us becomes a part of the family. You can say they were all family,' said Bindal.

'You will know that the kind of enmity you find in families is difficult to find elsewhere. The Mahabharat was also a fight in the family,' said Adhir.

Nitesh looked at him oddly.

'We have to talk to the servants also,' he said.

'And your son and daughter-in-law,' Adhir added.

The son and daughter-in-law were not home. The servants looked scared and answered questions timidly, but they did not seem to be hiding anything. The story remained the same. People had started arriving around eleven in the morning. The whole day people were in the house. They left only in the evening around four or five. Some even slept in the house.

Bhaiyaji was home and so was Bahuji. Alcohol flowed. Even the servants had had some. Yes, Parduman was here too.

They were about to leave when a white car entered the gate. They stopped in the verandah and looked at the servant who was escorting them out of the small sitting room. He said that this was the daughter-in-law, Saroj, who had brought her son home from school. A young boy got out of the back seat of the car and ran towards the side of the house, abandoning his school bag. The servant rushed to the car and picked up the school bag and whispered something to the woman in the car. She nodded and walked towards them, holding a small black clutch.

She is not beautiful, was Adhir's first thought. He always wondered why rich people married such women. Perhaps because they come from rich families. She was quite tall and wore a nearly white cotton sari with a thin gold zari border. Maybe the husband went out looking for sunflowers because he was tired of this lily at home, Adhirath thought. On her right wrist she had a watch on a leather strap with a white face and on her left wrist was a strap of some white metal. The half-moon ends of the metal strap were stapled together with some white stones. If they were diamonds they had not been cut like them—they looked like glass, like the industrial diamonds in kundan work that look like glass beads. Nothing glittered here, not even her eyes.

Taking measured steps, Saroj entered the small sitting room and placed her black purse on a tall carved stool. She sat down and pointed to the chairs in front of her.

'Go on,' she said looking at them with calm eyes.

Nitesh asked her about the farmhouse. A shadow passed over her eyes.

'It's been a year since I went there,' she said in measured tones.

'Earlier you used to go?' asked Adhir.

'A lot. Now there is a lot of work related to my son's school. *He* too is unwell,' she said using the pronoun to avoid naming her husband in the traditional way. 'Last year *he* got high blood sugar. We haven't been going to the farm.'

On the day of Holi, she told them, she was at home. You can't leave everything to the servants, can you? They were expecting nearly fifty guests. The sisters-in-law had not come; they had parties in their own homes. The son's friends celebrated Holi separately, in the basement, the elders did not even know that such a party was on. *He* had been home all day too. The driver arrived around noon. He had been called especially so that if any intoxicated guest wanted to leave he should be around to take them home. But he had to ferry only one guest. The Mamaji from Hauz Khas. Her mamiya sasur, her husband's uncle on his mother's side. He had had too much bhang. Left late in the afternoon. Around five-thirty or six. 'I had had a bed prepared for him so that he could sleep here. He could have gone the next day. But *he*,' she again used the pronoun to mean her husband, 'began to insist. Sometimes he really becomes very stubborn. He said what are we paying double rate to the driver for? To cool his heels here?'

Nitesh jotted down the number of the Hauz Khas-waale Mamaji.

Where was her husband that day?

'Here. Drank a lot. Must have been throwing up. Twice he rushed upstairs to the bathroom. Alcohol does not suit people with high blood sugar. Anyway, after helping Mamaji to the car, he shut himself in the room and slept so soundly, did not open the door for me, I kept knocking. I went to bed in the son's room, like this, in a sari. My nighties were all in the cupboard in the bedroom.'

Nitesh glanced at Adhir who leaned towards her and asked, 'What time did your husband get up in the morning?'

'Eight, at eight. When I came back after dropping my son to school the door to our room was still closed. Papaji went and knocked on it, then he opened it.'

For a while silence reigned in the room.

'Where is your husband now? In the factory?' asked Adhir.

'The factory shut down a year ago,' said Saroj rising from her chair, 'Ask him on the phone.' She gave them the husband's number.

Nitesh looked at Adhir as if to ask: 'Shall we finish with him too?'Adhir had stuffed himself with so many goodies all he wanted to do was take a nap. Nitesh leant against the Maruti Gypsy and called Udairaj on his mobile phone. He was in the club.

'Have to talk to you,' said Nitesh.

The answer he got swept away his yawn. 'Now,' he said sternly. 'Come to the police station.'

He added in a sterner voice. 'We don't have so much time.' Then he listened to what the man was saying, repeated the address of the club and switched off the phone.

'What was he saying?' asked Adhir.

'He was saying, "Go catch the murderer, why are you bothering decent people? When I have the time I will come and make my statement." Just look at his guts. That is why I said, "Come to the police thana right away." That set him straight. He lost some of his arrogance. Let us go and see what kind of club he is in, the bastard.'

The club was small. A few chairs were scattered on the lawn

and some people were chatting away. The doorman saluted them but looked a bit perplexed and hesitated to let them enter. A man sat behind a small table inside the door and stood up the moment he saw them.

'Whom do you want to meet?' he asked. Had Nitesh not been in uniform it would have been difficult to gain entry thought Adhir.

'That Udairaj,' said Nitesh.

'Your name?' asked the man, pulling the register towards him.

'Police,' barked Nitesh, 'Where is Udairaj?'

He was venting his anger at Udairaj on this minion.

The man's demeanour changed dramatically. He folded his hands. 'Just doing my job, sir,' he said apologetically. Then he got out from behind the table and said, 'Come, this way sir,' and led them to an inner room where he went up to a man sitting alone at a table and announced that his guests had arrived. Whether it was because the man had nearly prostrated himself, or the sight of the obviously expensive furniture—the shadows thrown by the tasteful lampshades and the tinkling chandelier inside the room—Adhirath didn't know, but Nitesh cooled down. The display of wealth works like a fire fighter indeed.

'Yes, yes, put it down to me in the bill,' Udairaj said to the man waving at the chairs across the table in a gesture asking them to sit down. 'They charge you for the entry of guests and this man is truly fussy about it. Welcome, Inspector sahib, what will you have to drink? Please, make yourselves comfortable.' He had a red drink in a square glass before him that was half empty.

Udairaj seemed to have dressed with great care. Adhirath had seen a number of expensive shirts but this shirt was in a league of its own. Each thread bore testimony to the care taken over the weave, the cut, the finish. This was not a shirt available in shops that ordinary mortals went to. Its colour was a yellow so pale it looked transparent.

Udairaj did not stand up but what they could see of him suggested that he was tall and lean. His face was easy on the eyes. His eyebrows were even, his lips full. His short hair had been gelled to attention. His face was free of blemishes and the skin smooth. His nails were clipped neatly, not the type of uneven clipping a nail cutter gives you at home. Did he go to a parlour? There are parlours for men nowadays, so Adhirath had heard. The days of the barber's shop at the corner and their vigorous oil massage of the head was over. Udairaj was clearly metrosexual.

Adhirath stared at his glass. What was he drinking? He had come in thinking the man would have some golden fluid in a glass before him, but here it was something else. Red like thin blood. Looked like tomato juice. The rim of the glass had a line of salt around it, like the thin border of a sari. A little salt must tickle the tongue with every sip. Adhirath felt the taste of salt on his tongue.

'Will you have a drink? Scotch? It's over the yardarm somewhere in the world,' Udairaj said lifting his glass to his lips. 'This is a Bloody Mary, tomato juice and vodka. Want some?'

A waiter manifested, pad ready, pen poised. Perhaps he had seen that the rich member had guests. Perhaps it was the khaki uniform.

'We are on duty,' said Nitesh.

Adhirath thought: I am not on duty. I could easily down two Scotches. It would be good to find out whether the fire of expensive whisky was different. He had never tasted Scotch, not even an inexpensive one, not even when he had his post. This crorepati must be used to very sophisticated Scotch. Udairaj ordered nimbu pani, kababs, and various other delicacies.

'The chicken adraki here is very tasty. All my Jain friends eat it here. The club has been set up for this purpose only. At home we can't have even garlic,' said Udairaj, with a faint smile.

'You know, don't you, that there has been a murder at your farmhouse?' Nitesh said. 'The formal statement will only be recorded when you visit the police station. You have to sign it.'

Udairaj nodded. The waiter arrived and began arranging plates on the table. Adhirath noticed that Udairaj had turned his eyes to Nitesh with a mute appeal in them to not broach the subject of murder in the presence of the waiter. They kept quiet till the waiter had left.

'You want to know where I was on the day of Holi?'

It was now Nitesh's turn to smile. 'How do you know?'

Udairaj also smiled. Just then the waiter arrived with the eats. Udairaj's phone rang, playing the tune of some English song. He fished out the phone from the top pocket of his shirt and disconnected it.

'Who was it?' asked Adhirath helping himself to a wafer-thin slice of cucumber.

'A friend,' said Udairaj and went silent on them for a minute or so. When the waiter began to leave, Udairaj told him not to disturb them at all and to come only when called. His voice had the authority of a man used to issuing orders and being obeyed.

The waiter bowed slightly and effaced himself.

'Start from where you were going to. Where were you on the day of Holi?'

'Actually, I shouldn't be here drinking again. I had had enough at the party. I was at home. I did not eat bhang pakoras.

Don't like bhang. But if there is liquor in front of me, I find it hard to control my hands. I keep pouring. I had a lot. Next thing I was in the bedroom with the door closed. Must have passed out. Saroj says she banged the door a lot but I did not open. Father woke me up, in the morning.'

'You did not get up even once?'Adhirath asked placing the bone he had picked clean of the chicken adraki back on an empty quarter plate.

Udairaj's eyes narrowed a little. Running his fingers through the hair around his temples, he said: 'Maybe once or twice. I felt very restless. I even stepped out on the balcony. Went downstairs also, took some deep breaths in the fresh air. Then back to the bed. And lights out.'

'Did you know the girl?' Nitesh asked, fixing his gaze on Udairaj's face.

'Yes, everybody knew her. Meaning, we knew she was some relative of Parduman. But not enough to talk to her.'

'When was the last time you visited the farm?'

Adhirath felt that the question had alerted Udairaj. Drumming on his temple with his index finger and the middle finger, Udairaj sank into thought. Then he shrugged, 'Don't remember.'

'Well make a guess. On Holi? Bhang grows wild there. Perhaps you went to bring some for the party?'

'Oh, I never do any of that. Papa used to get it from the farm. Don't know if he got it from there this year too.'

He seemed a clever man, Adhirath thought. Well, he did run a business, didn't he? Do people who drink enough to vomit at night look so fresh in the morning? Do they down more liquor? Once or twice, he too had had too much to drink, but the next day his eyes refused to open. If he opened them light pierced them like a spear. Darkness brought very little comfort. In fact, nothing brought comfort. One's head was like a rock and hung loosely on the neck. This guy looked bathed, groomed, fresh and crisp.

'So when did you go to the farm last?' Adirath asked.

'I can't recall. Must have been a month or two ago. Really, I can't remember.'

'Had I had a farm I would eat only the vegetables grown on it,' Nitesh said closely examining a slim roundel of tomato.

'It makes no difference to me. That is Saroj's department.'

Nitesh's perfunctory interrogation made it clear that he did not think Udairaj had anything to do with this murder. But he had been trained to treat everyone as a suspect. They had had this drilled into their heads at the academy: everyone is guilty until proved innocent. That was the way to solve a crime.

They munched on, all three lost in thought. The waiter brought in fresh rotis. Another Bloody Mary had also arrived. Noticing Adhirath stare at the brimming glass, Udairaj said, 'Only iron can cut iron.'

'That driver of yours. Where is he?' Nitesh asked.

'He was on duty on Holi. Since then he has absented himself. Must be at home,' Udairaj replied calmly.

His gaze was fixed on the glass, his eyes lowered, it was difficult to gauge his reaction, but the answer was so prompt, it appeared to have been a practiced one, as if he was waiting for the question. When Nitesh asked for Parduman's address Udairaj rested his head on his palm and closed his eyes.

'Some jhilak milak it is called. Somewhere near Vivek Vihar. I have given him a mobile phone. I'll give you the number. Or else I will ask Saroj and let you know the address.'

Well, the ways of the rich are unique, thought Adhirath

who used his mobile phone with great care, finding a landline wherever possible. The government had not yet issued mobile phones to all ranks of the police. Only the top officers had them, not the lower ranks. And here Udairaj's driver had a mobile phone; the boss clearly picked up the tab.

There was no jhilak milak, nothing sparkling, about Jhilmil Colony. Narrow lanes, overflowing sewage, large potholes, open manholes. A constable could have been sent. The driver could have been asked to report to the police station. But Nitesh wanted to make a trip to Jhilmil Colony.

'That is where Dalchand lives, doesn't he? Let's meet him,' he had said to Adhirath. They could have gone back to his police station. At night, Nitesh could have asked the man to come to the thana and questioned him at leisure. Those they wanted to question only cursorily, had been met.

'Everyone speaks only when kicked around, but there are people you can't kick, it boomerangs; you can break your own legs,' Adhirath used to say. That is why cases in which the poor are suspects are cracked so easily. Who can endure the interrogation techniques of the police and keep denying involvement in a crime? You raise a hand and the confession is out the next minute.

'The bloody courts have spoiled it all. Had it been left to the police alone so many crimes would have been controlled by now, no?' asked Nitesh. 'Should we go to Dalchand's first?'

This annoyed Adhirath. He had not wanted to meet Dalchand. Everyone was bent upon reminding him of the one thing he wanted to forget. At home and outside too.

'No use, what can he do?' Adhirath asked with some asperity.

'Yaar, you put the noose around your neck for him. He will do something. Even if he gets his lawyer to talk to us, it will be something. The enquiry will be held soon.'

'In the morning didn't you say you had no news about it?' Adhirath asked, his anger distending his face and creeping into his voice.

'Arre, there is no news, but it has been over a year. How long can it be postponed?'

Adhirath kept quiet. The steering wheel of the jeep was in Nitesh's hands. Even Pushpa has been saying the same thing: Go talk to the guy for whom you risked your job. It was not as if Adhirath had not spoken to him. That very day Dalchand had come to him and remarked, 'What have you done Janaab?'

Truly, what had he done? It should have been obvious that Dalchand would defend himself. Or else he would pay for his actions. Adhirath's head would begin to spin whenever he thought that he would have to pay for Dalchand's actions. What a system! Nobody stands up for you. Pushpa is right, the police may be a huge institution but everyone inside it is alone and even among them 'people like us' are even more alone. Nobody will defend us. Nobody will promote us on schedule. Nobody will give us a good posting. And if you do find something good, everyone will try to pull you down.

Dalchand's house was right in front of them but they had to find a parking space first. After three rounds of the market, Nitesh edged the front wheels of the Gypsy onto a couple of Kota stones covering a drain and parked his jeep. He got out, cursing the place loudly. All around were small kiosks selling plastic flowers, and children's party frocks made of nylon and netting. As they walked up the lane, a paranda caressed Nitesh's face. It was draped on a rope slung across two ends of the kiosk.

Shoving it away Nitesh stopped in his tracks and stared at this length of black threads, which young women wove into their plaits to make their hair look longer and more luscious, ending in bright, tantalizing tassels that they flung around while flirting with men.

'Yaar, look, they still have these things,' he said, truly surprised.

'I had completely forgotten there was such a thing!'

Dalchand was at home. He was lying on a cot in a banian and lungi, with a remote in one hand. Nowadays, no man who is home does anything but watch TV. He leapt to his feet when he saw the two enter, and grabbing a shirt hanging on a nail from behind the door, put it on. He muttered a 'Namaste' and went back to sit on the cot. By the time his wife got them tea, Dalchand was at ease.

'Only yesterday, Janaab, yesterday I had a hearing. Till now there have been eight,' he said. He handed the cups of tea to them. 'What can I say, sir, I feel terrible. Till yesterday I used to take criminals to court and today I stand in their place. They call out my name, I go in, mark my attendance and come back. Nothing else has happened till now. Only attendance. Appearance. The lawyer says it is good. The more time it takes for the trial to begin the greater the chance that the memory of the witnesses will weaken. What do you say, Janaab, do you think I will be acquitted? Nobody from the department has even come to enquire about it or find out if I am alive or dead.'

Dalchand seemed in dire financial straits. 'The Missus has joined as an ayah in a school, somehow we make do,' he said when he saw them scan the room with open curiosity. Taken aback, they lowered their eyes. On top of it, he had to pay the lawyer's fees and shoulder the other expenses in court. Has the spine of his wife too grown stiff with arrogance? Adhirath wondered and immediately kicked himself for thinking such thoughts.

'Tell me something, Janaab, I rescued the whole area from that goon. Was it a crime?'

'Look, Dalchand, there is a system in place. By the way, why did you do it?' Nitesh asked. 'Tell us the truth. What is there to hide from friends?'

'I lost my head, what else?' said Dalchand but his eyes were glued to the floor.

They all knew that it was not so simple. Whatever had happened that day had not come as a bolt from the blue.

Dalchand still remembers that day, like it was yesterday. The sun blazed down harshly so that even your shadow huddled beneath your feet. The whole thing took place in a blind alley though Dalchand could never figure out why they called it that. The lanes called blind alleys have thousands of eyes glued to the cracks in the walls on both sides, eyes that watch everything, see nothing. The windows had closed almost immediately after the shots rang out. Windows with soiled and torn curtains, windows with newspapers rustling over the panes, windows with rotting wooden planks for panes, all sorts of windows, all of them closed one by one. What better proof of the presence of all those eyes that had watched everything but saw nothing?

Dalchand had not forgotten for he depended on the mercy of those people. The lawyer had told him to not talk to anyone, to say nothing to anyone.

'You know...if we can be of any help, let us know,' Adhirath said. Nitesh had truly got him into a nice mess now.

'You do know that there is an enquiry pending against him?' Nitesh said pointing to Adhir.

'Hasn't happened yet? Who knows? The delay may do you good,' said Dalchand.

'Listen, Dalchand, they will ask you also,' Adhir said. 'Just side with me, yaar...that is all we had come to say.'

Dalchand remained silent. There are very few who will come rushing to the rescue of a subordinate. When he had worked with Adhirath, he had found him quite decent. True, he could not bring himself to respect the softness of Adhirath's heart. Everybody in the thana said the man had very little manhood in him. And though Dalchand felt a sneaking sympathy for Adhirath, he acknowledged that the man was unsuited to the force.

'Have to ask the lawyer,' Dalchand mumbled.

'Ask,' said Nitesh promptly, 'Here take my phone and ask.'

Dalchand said that he would not talk on the phone.

'So let us go meet him,' Nitesh said. 'Listen yaar, we all belong to the same comoonity. We have to stand by each other. He also did what he did with the same intention, to help one's own. Here, give me the number, I will call the lawyer.'

Adhirath was moved to tears. He suddenly felt light. How lucky that he had gone to meet Nitesh. But Dalchand demurred, saying that the lawyer might not be in his office.

'The court must have closed by now,' Nitesh said.

'You know, the court closes only when the judge wants it to,' said Dalchand, trying to get rid of them.

But Nitesh did not return the phone to his pocket; he kept it waving in front of Dalchand's eyes, a challenge to do something for the officer who had rushed to his help. At last, Dalchand dug out a diary and read out a number.

The lawyer was sitting in his office.

'I had told you, remember, sir, about the officer who had tried to help me, had I not? They are here to meet me. They want to meet you,' Dalchand said to the lawyer.

The lawyer asked them to come 'at this time' three days later.

3

Chandola was on the way to Amirpur. Adhirath wondered whether he had come to get the radish he could not pull out that day or to run away from the honking of motorcars, so that he might soak up the silence of this place. When Adhir neared Chandola, his mobike slowed. Today he noticed a a small room standing a little away from the road with a plastic chair in it. On its wall was scrawled '*Proparty Agent*' in white. A man sat on a high pile of neatly arranged bricks, picking his teeth. Adhir came to a halt there.

'Ram Ram,' he said to the bored-looking man. The man nodded and climbing down, brought out the chair. Beating the dust on the seat of the chair with his bare hands, he said, 'Sit down, sahib.' He then fetched a glass and a plastic jug which might have been red when new. He rinsed the glass with a little water from the jug, and then filled it to the brim and handed Adhir a glass of tepid water. He told Adhir that his name was Bharat and could get him a 'very nice plot'. 'The paroparty market is hotting up now, in a year, two will become four.'

'I am indeed looking for some land here,' said Adhirath.

Pointing to the vacant land next to his room Bharat said, 'Take this plot. Road touch. Fifty yards. You can get a pelot of hundred yards also. Only two pelots have been sold till now.

Just take your pick. Will measure you one wherever you want.'

'Not this. Something bigger. Say four acres?' Adhir said thinking that the farmhouse he wished to inspect was about that large. Suddenly he realized that it was this wish for inspection that had brought his motorcycle to a halt. Bharat smiled very faintly. Had his eyes not been fixed on his face, Adhir would not have seen the smile. Bharat was now looking at his motorcycle. All of a sudden Adhir looked at his own bike from the view point of Bharat. The black paint was rubbing off. The box that he used to keep things in had many scratches. It looked old and much used.

'Land rates are going up sharply,' Bharat said. 'Had you come even a year ago you could have got four keele (acres) in fifteen-sixteen lakhs. Now the rate has climbed up to eight lakhs for one keela. It won't be less than thirty-two lakhs.'

Adhir smiled. 'Thirty-two or thirty-five, what difference does it make to the rich? They don't even have the time to go looking for land. They hire people like us.'

'Ohhoo, so you are also from our line? Should have said so.' This time Bharat laughed with genuine pleasure.

'No, no,' Adhir said, 'I work in their office. Getting stuff from the market. Carrying cash. Things like that. The work needs someone trustworthy.'

Bharat was now alert. There was land for sale close by, he told Adhirath; he would take him there. They mounted the bike again, Bharat sitting pillion, and rode down the silent, empty road. On both sides there was so much land lying vacant that Adhir began to feel surprised. Clumps of tall grass with blades sharp as razors grew on them. At one place, he saw some bushes in very glossy green, the type he had seen sitting in plastic buckets at the florists. Glittering green fronds of feathery leaves—to be added to bouquets for free. He always used to think that the florists dipped them in paint. Now he was surprised to see that the fluorescent green was their natural colour.

'What is this?' he asked Bharat.

'This? We call it jhund. In days gone by they used to thatch roofs with this grass. Now they use concrete. Its blades are very sharp. It can cut your fingers.'

'No, no, not that grass. That other bush, the very green one.' But they had left those bushes behind.

'Must be some wild grass,' said Bharat carelessly.

Having taken a round of the place, they returned to Bharat's room. Bharat had shown him two pieces of land, one was nearly three acres big, the other was about two acres. The larger one was a little away from the road and a narrow pathway led to it.

'Will find out about more pelots and let you know,' Bharat said.

'These pieces are too close to the village, they won't like it,' said Adhir. Looking around he pointed to the iron gate of the farmhouse on which elephants still stood with garlands in their trunks.

'What is that?' Adhir asked.

'That too is up for sale. But it is very big, could be nineteen acres,' said Bharat.

'Well, show it to me at least.'

Bharat began to scrape his nails.

'Let me tell you the truth. I have never seen so much land in my life. Can't we see it? Who knows, the owner may sell it, piece by piece?'

Now Adhir was beginning to regret that he had asked for only a four-acre plot. How would he know that such a narrow path could lead to a large expanse of land? Frankly, he did not even know how much an acre was. Just now when he saw the three acre plot, that is when he began to get some idea of how much it could be.

'They won't sell it in pieces. They need a huge amount of money.' They both walked to the gate. 'If the guard is there he will show it to us. Are you from Delhi?'

'Yes. And you are from this very village? Chandola?'

'No, I am from Bahadurgarh. Came for business. There the rates have crossed the capacity of every pocket. Builders have started camping there. Most of the land is already sold. Rates of all places nearby are also on fire. Here it is still cool. There aren't too many dealers too. And since rates here too are high, one can make a decent commission.'

Bharat called out for the chowkidar at the gate, 'Chetilal, oye, Cheti.' There was no response. Bharat inserted his hand between the rods of the gate, found the bolt and slid it open. Right in front of them was the house that could only hang as a picture frame on the wall of Adhir's house. After about two hundred metres, the land opened up. Adhirath then knew that what was visible from the road was only a small portion of the house. It did not even face the road, its face was towards the east, on his left. In front was a wide lawn. A marble fountain. A wide verandah stood behind pillars of sandstone. Adhirath was astonished to see that even the door and window frames were made of stone.

'People spend lakhs on building houses in which nobody lives,' Bharat said. 'And millions don't have a roof over their heads, hai na?'

On the other side of the house, from where the gate could not be seen, there was more land. Adhirath thought the land looked endless. A small pond stood behind the house as the border between the garden and the rest of the land. It was made of a cement tank sunk into the ground and broad leaves floated on its surface. A pipe jutted out of the pond.

'It is attached to a small motor. They suck the water out to water the plants,' said Bharat. 'Then fill up the pond again. Everything was planned carefully. They take a lot of care of the place.'

'They are growing lotus,' Adhir tried to display his knowledge.

'It has blue flowers.'

'Neel Kamal! I used to think that Neel Kamal is only a myth.'

'Here everything is unique. Now it is in ruins. You should have seen it earlier. Even the cauliflowers they grew here were green. You have seen a pumpkin, no? Our pumpkins are round, aren't they? These people had long ones. With very smooth skin, with spots on them, faint spots.'

Three mulberry trees formed a triangle near the pond and the ground beneath was mushy with the fallen fruit on which were stuck fat ants and even fatter honey bees, grown lethargic with the excess of food. The dead body had been found in this very triangle but Adhirath did not know this. He sighed deeply. Why would anyone want to sell such a calm and beautiful place? Till the eyes could see, there was land. A vast field of dry yellowish stalks, the remainders of harvested mustard. Yellow and reddish marigolds were planted near the house in complete disorder. In a corner the purple hue of alyssum sparkled. He looked around. On his right were bushes of the same fluorescent green foliage he no longer wanted to know the name of. A bird called.

'Allah teri kudrat,' Bharat said. Adhir looked at him with curiosity. 'That is what the bird says. Black partridge. Every day in the afternoon it calls. Must be standing somewhere on the wall here.'

This time even Adhirath thought that the bird was complaining 'Allah teri kudrat'. The teetar speaks Urdu! He turned his head from one side to another to catch a glimpse of the famous bird that he had only heard of. A grey hare emerged from the green bushes and ran into the nearby bushes shaking its ears.

'They get to eat all the fruits here,' said Bharat. He shook a branch and the ripe, nearly black mulberry rained on the ground.

'Will you believe me if I told you that only a few days ago a girl's body was found here? The entire village came to see. That is why nobody has eaten any of this fruit. The policemen did not even taste it.' He raised his arm again to the branch but Adhirath caught it preventing him from shaking the tree. Grass did not grow under the trees. Red blotches were scattered over the ground below. It was difficult to tell the blood from the juice of the overripe fruit. Adhirath picked some fruit from a low branch, there were bees sticking to them and he had to shake them off.

'I would never sell this place if I owned it,' Adhir remarked. His eyes, trained to look for signs of crime, also failed to distinguish between mulberry stains and blood stains beneath the trees. The soil was red. At one place it had been dug up a little. The police must have taken a sample from there. 'Please don't shake the tree. We never get a chance to pluck fruit from trees,' he said.

'They are selling because they need the money. They used

to make TV parts. Had a factory in Noida. That shut down. It is happening to a lot of people, businesses are closing down. Land—that is real wealth. What is in a factory? It can be locked up. A lot of people are selling their factories to forners. So I have heard. It is also possible that these people may have some family dispute, brothers dividing up property. Maybe they have to clear a debt. Who knows what it is? Earlier they did not have the time to come here, now they have all the time in the world but the land will not be theirs.'

Adhirath nodded. The mulberries were melting in his mouth, unbelievably sweet. Had he bought them, he would have thought that the fruit-seller had dipped them in syrup. When he was a child, women would come to sell them in small baskets lined with fresh mulberry leaves, the red fruit looking like piles of ants with an unripe fruit winking greenly from the heap. His grandfather, his Nanaji of beloved memory, called them 'jalebe'. Truly, they were like jalebi. He resolved to take a bagful home.

He looked around. The teetar had fallen silent. Something glinted on the ground. He bent and picked it up. Glass. A bit of blue glass, too thick for a bangle, too wide, part of a bracelet? It had two tiny white glass beads embedded on it. He turned it around, studying it. When he looked up, he found Bharat was studying him. They would have to leave now. He would have to find a way to come here alone.

'The chowkidar is enjoying all this. Where is he?' asked Adhir in an attempt to cover up. 'He could have given us a plastic bag to carry some fruit.'

As they turned to leave, Adhir could not resist a last look. Vasantmalti laughed on the walls. There was another creeper that had saffron flowers, a plant whose name he did not know. Through a crack in a dusty window, he could look into a room, a bedroom perhaps? Yes, there was a four-poster with a dark blue dust sheet. Against the wall, a dressing table in the same wood with an oval swinging mirror. Two more chairs. The furniture looked antique. Adhirath could not tell whether they were real or well-designed fakes. He was amazed that people could furnish houses and not live in them. He had heard of such farmhouses but it was a different thing to see one.

A squirrel scampered down from the terrace and the motion caught his attention. His gaze followed her flight through the garden and he noticed a piece of yellow cloth and a glint of something golden. They were partially covered by the yellow soil. He casually pulled out his handkerchief from his pocket, mopped his forehead. Then pretending to tie his shoelaces, he bent down and swept up the golden thing and the yellow piece of cloth in his kerchief. A small length of yellow red string trailed behind the golden thing. Shoving his handkerchief in his pocket, he caught up with Bharat who was striding ahead.

'They are asking for a little more than the going market rate,' Bharat said. 'You have seen how narrow the access road is. If they divide it, how will they give access to the other guy? In a village you have to give everyone access to their field. The land next to this piece is inami land. You know what that means? It is land that was given as a gift to someone. It cannot be sold or bought. So you can't buy access from there. There are ways of doing it but it is complicated. Even then, let me enquire what they have to say. Had the chowkidar been around, I would've got the owner's number. Could have called right away. Must have gone to the thana.'

'Thana? Why?'

Bharat looked at him again. 'Told you, they found a body here.'

'Oh, yes. I had completely forgotten. Who was she? The owner's daughter?'

Bharat laughed uproariously. 'She was from a village close by. Not a good girl either. Otherwise what does a village girl have to do with a farmhouse? She was a pross. It said so in the papers too.'

'Oh, so this is that farm,' Adhirath cried in mock surprise. 'Then it is different. Who will touch land that is involved in a police case?'

'The police is not going to camp here forever. These are rich people. The police will get money out of them, line their pockets and bury the matter. Am I right or am I correct?'

Adhirath mumbled something non-committal. If his hair had not grown out and his stride returned to normal, Bharat would have had no trouble recognizing him as a policeman. But was he right? Did Nitesh stand to make a lakh or two over this case?

'It is a murder. They will have to catch the culprit.'

'She was a pross. This is how prosses end up,' said Bharat. 'She used to keep coming here. The whole village knew. This is not a city. Everyone knows who comes and goes in a village.'

'And the villagers allowed her to do her business?' Adhirath asked.

'She came here. It is a faramhouse. Whoever the owner allows can come. What can villagers say?' They had reached Bharat's room of the not-very-straight walls. Bharat patted a chair, inviting him to sit down.

'Looks like we shall become good friends,' said Adhirath. 'Now I must take your leave. Had there been a polythene bag, I would have gathered some mulberries.'

Bharat got the hint. He went inside and found an empty

plastic container from a restaurant. He brought it out, rinsed it with the water from the jug and told Adhirath that last week he had bought some korma and it had come in that box. Thin white plastic that would crack with a second use. 'This will do well for the shahtoot,' he added.

Adhirath nodded.

'This murder-shurder...' he began.

'Listen, this is not an affair of the village. These city people, they build houses on khets and live in them. Nobody in the village does this. They live away from the farms in a specific place. All together, close to each other and everyone knows what is going on in the other's house. But faramhouses, they are on khets. The villagers don't have anything to do with them. They don't interfere but they keep an eye on things, they know everything.'

'This is very useful. The police will benefit from this.'

Once again Bharat laughed aloud. Slapping Adhirath's back, he said, 'Come over some day. We shall catch some rabbits and roast them. Have a party. The villagers never tell an outsider anything.'

'At least they will give us the number of the farmhouse owner,' said Adhirath joining in his laughter.

'Then they will also ask for a cut in the deal. You can't trust anyone in this business,' Bharat said. 'Am I right or am I correct?'

Another man who had lost his trust in his fellow beings, Adhirath thought and mounted his bike.

It was easy to find the Kiliopetra Parlour. The difficult thing was to escape the notice of the policemen in the thana. The parlour was almost opposite the police station. Adhirath rode past the thana and took a turn at random and parked his bike. Then he fished out a cap from the box on his bike and pulled it down over his forehead. Then he retraced his steps, while examining his recently acquired booty.

The yellow cloth appeared to be the corner of a dupatta. The golden thing was a button. Two discs of gold, one smaller than the other held together with a slim stem of gold. The larger disc was studded with a sparkling stone. Was it a diamond? Or glass? He held it to the sunlight. The stone glittered inscrutably. It said nothing to his uneducated eye. As he was about to enter the parlour, a girl stepped up and tried to shut the door.

'Sir, for ladies only,' she said.

He stuck a foot in and said, 'I want to talk about Renu. You know the police...'

The word 'police' electrified the girl; she gave up defending the space and fled. He stepped into a room which had five swivel chairs facing five mirrors. Each of the chairs was occupied by a woman: one had her face covered in a blue paste, another had a white paste all over her arms, the third had her feet on a towel and a girl working industriously on her toes. The girl returned from an inner room and said he had been summoned within.

A senior woman greeted him there. 'Myself, Mrs Malik,' she said and folded her hands. 'We have made our statements to the police yesterday, how many questions baba and how many hours. Now you have come again during our business hours. How are we to eat? Good you came in plain clothes. But when you talk about Renu, it will worry the cushtumbers...'

'Doesn't look like you're hurting,' said Adhir.

The woman shrugged and pointed at the skies above. The Kiliopetra Parlour had benefited from the news about Renu.

New customers were arriving and the regulars were now coming earlier to get their mani-pedi.

'I am not from the police,' Adhirath said. 'I am a relative of the girl. I wanted to see her stuff. Chachi was asking for it. Her mother. Poor woman. If you wish I can get someone from the thana to come here as my witness.'

The veiled threat had the desired effect. For the next half hour he sat with the owner, drinking tea. He told Mrs Malik that his aunt had named his cousin Suryabala, but the inspector had told him that she lived here under the assumed name of Renu. The girl was dead for them for all practical purposes, he said. Now all that was left was to be done with the last rites and to bathe in the Ganga, because the birth of such a girl itself is a sin from which there is no escape for the family.

'Twice, twice my poor aunt got her married off but she could not wash her sins away, could she? Such a bad character that girl was,' Adhirath said stressing every syllable and touching both his ears with his hands; he was playing at being Bharat, using his accent and intonations.

'She was not like that,' said Mrs Malik, incensed. 'You people look at parlour work with wrong eyes. We don't do anything bad; it is honest work. Your sister wanted to live the way she wanted to. She would have married someone too of her own choice. Which woman doesn't want to have a home and children? You will all say, parlour girls are like this, parlour girls do like that, but when there is marriage in family, all come here, all send sisters and daughters here to get bridal done. Why? Why call us to the home for make-up? If we are so bad, why trust us with your sisters and daughters?'

Adhirath said that this might be so in the cities but in the village, traditions still held, even now they put turmeric on the bride at home only.

Mrs Malik sniffed a loud and disbelieving sniff. 'Oh fau, they say and you believe. Women from Amirpur, Chandola, Jhandapur, and so many other villages come here to get facial. Facial is not for anyone to do. You have to know how to do. You think all these brides look so nice from eating carrots or what?'

She was off again: 'The daughter-in-law of the pardhan of Chandola comes here every month with her mother-in-law. She is the one who went and told the village folk that Renu works in this parlour. She always got Renu to do pedicure. Always. Once she was saying: come to my house and do it. Renu said no. I had to talk to them, make them understand that our girls don't go to people's houses on their own. If you want things done at home we go as a team and you have to send the car to take us and to bring us back. We keep all security for our girls. Here, Rakhi has come. Rakhi, take him to Renu's room.'

The room was a low-ceilinged space mezzanine, squashed between two floors. Dozens of cardboard boxes were stacked against the wall, some of which were open. They were full of cans and bottles of make-up. He thought of the Solah Shringar, the sixteen ways in which a woman beautified herself. He would often wonder: how could they have found so many different things with which to scrub and wash and massage and paint and perfume their bodies? But in this small, stuffy room, he was surrounded by stuff used to improve the looks of women, these tubes and bottles were the descendants of the unguents and mixtures of old.

There was a folding bed on one side with a thin mattress on it, two trunks shoved under it. Inside the trunks, expensive clothes, not outfits picked up from the weekly Budh Bazaar, not even export surplus stuff. Even if the police had taken some of it away, what was left looked expensive. There were two-three purses too, rexine—made to look like leather. They were empty.

Adhirath lifted the clothes out of the trunk, one after another. There was a lehenga with tassels hanging from the long tapes used to tie it up. It was the brightest dress in the trunk. There were three skirts that were hybrids between skirts and lehangas. And five salwar kameez. He hesitated to touch the inner wear, some with lace, others of netting. He glanced at Rakhi, hoping she would help him turn these over but she lowered her eyes. He shook out every lehanga, every salwar, every kurta and dupatta, turned each pocket inside out, ran his fingers in every purse, upturned them on his palms but found nothing.

Handing a purse to Rakhi he said, 'Maybe you know if there is a secret compartment in it. I can't find what I am looking for.'

'What are you looking for?' she asked.

Adhirath had no reply so he asked: 'You lived with her?'

'She lived alone. My home is nearby only,' Rakhi said with a frown. 'My family knows what I do. And my brother, no, he only brings me here and takes me back to the house also.'

'Then you will not know,' he said.

'We talked lots,' Rakhi said. Her curiosity was aroused.

'Even then she would not tell you secrets. Things that one keeps in the stomach,' said Adhir, using a local phrase to pique her curiosity.

They hedged and danced around for a while until Rakhi asked him outright what he wanted to know. 'Women talk to each other, sir. She might have told me her secrets. She knew I could keep them in my stomach.'

They fenced for a while until Rakhi could bear no more and said he might ask her anything he wanted, for who knew, she might actually have been told some secrets? 'Anyways, what is there to lose? I am not going to tell anyone what we have talked about. I can keep secrets.'

Adhirath sat down on the cot and said in a resigned tone, 'I was thinking that I will give it to my old chachi; she could have something to hold on to. One day she had called me, my cousin. She said on the phone that someone had given her something very expensive, a diamond. She wanted to make a ring. I work for goldsmith, no, that is why she had called me. She was saying it was like a button. But I can't find it here. May be the police found it and took it away. Did the police take it?'

'Was it truly diamond? She had shown it to me. It was a button. Looked like gold. She always kept it in the purse. Always.'

'I could have told if I had seen it. How do I know if it was diamond or not?'

'It could have been. The man who gave it to her, he came in this big a car,' she said spreading her arms apart to indicate the size of the car, 'with driver. He took her with him. She would be sitting next to him. Very tall. But he was married. I said to her, what will you gain? What is the use? It is not like he will marry you. She used to say he will always keep her. She said she had got him addicted.'

'Addicted? To what?' Adhirath asked taken aback. But Rakhi shook her head.

'That she did not tell,' said Rakhi.

Adhirath began to ask about the button again saying maybe the police found it.

'Police may have found it, who knows? I and Malik auntie, we both brought the police here. But we did not see the police take away anything like that. But you know, we were not watching everything that police was doing. That button, no, it was always in her purse. One day I only told her that she should make it a ring because the purse can also be stolen. That is why she must have thought about it.'

Adhirath ran his hands over the bottom of the empty trunk. 'Do you remember what she was wearing that day?'

Rakhi said that they had all gone to the temple on the day before Holi and there the pujari had tied strings on their wrists. By the time Holika was burnt at night Rakhi had returned home so she did not know what happened after that.

'Every Holi and Diwali, the pujari ties the thread. It is red and yellow thread plaited together. You must know what it is. She was going to be at home on Holi. I did not come at all so I don't know what she was wearing. When we left the mandir, that was last time I saw her.'

Adhirath stuffed the dresses back in one of the two trunks and began to climb down with it, but before taking the stairs he turned to her and said, 'Rakhi, do you want any of these dresses? What will Chachi do with them? It is no use to her. If you want, take one or two.'

Rakhi refused to take even one of them.

It was late by the time he got home. Buses were queued up on the roads and two-wheelers wove their way from between them like cockroaches. The cacophony was unbearable: a chorus of voices screaming: 'Look at us, nobody cares two hoots about us at home, in the office, but here we are, here we exist, look at us, see us, get out of our way or else.' The sweetness of the mulberry, the enjoyment of his conversation with Bharat, the anticipation of a peg of rum at home, everything evaporated in the cacophony. If a person were being murdered here you wouldn't hear the screams. He knew he wouldn't find peace even at home. The house sat on the road, a platform of bricks on which walls had been raised to separate it from the street, to justify calling it a house. His father had bought this small plot from the DDA—a single room on some fifty square yards. Later, they had built another room on top. The stairs were outside in the lane that doubled as a community courtyard. A far cry from homes in Hindi films where a curving flight of stairs inside the drawing room led to the bedrooms upstairs. Here, they lived on the street. Everyone could see them going up and down. All round the house was a uniform ugliness—rectangular rooms, jaundiced walls, windows that did not close properly, dusty screen doors that remained open through the day...

Even before he stepped in, he heard Bhikulal's monologue inside the house.

'The thickness of fingers, the colour of the arm, you have to recognize everything. Then you match them...just put any two parts together. Pack them in a bag and hand it over. Which sasura is looking to see if the hand is actually that of the man from his family or what...counted the dead by counting the hands? Every hand I counted. That is how we got to know how many died. Otherwise do you think the police would have been able to figure out how many died? You can't trust people; they tell you four died when only two have been killed... In the end everything is just a handful of dust. We all come from the earth and have to go back to the earth. Even if you get someone else's remains in a bag, you perform the rites and are at peace that you have done all that is necessary. Who checks if the remains are of the person they lost? You just assume that it is and are at peace...fifty people will come to claim that they have also lost someone. Give us compensation, they will say. It is a task of great responsibility. Have to count piroperly and keep all record. I found two right hands only. Only right hands. The left hands may have been blown away. At least you got the clean hand for the rites...'

Adhirath stood at the door wondering why the man had come today? He was lucky to have arrived at the end of the narration of the story of the bomb blast. He would not repeat the story now. Mamaji only told the story once a day. Adhirath ran upstairs, slid the trunk under the bed and sauntered back.

'Here he comes,' his father, Daulatram, said. 'You don't know how long he has been waiting for you. Where have you been going nowadays? Running around all day,' the smile on his face stayed put though his eyes narrowed a little.

'Paaon laagoon, Mamaji,' Adhirath said.

'Only verbally? Do it properly, bend and touch his feet. Or stop pretending to keep the custom,' Daulatram admonished him.

Adhirath placed the half bottle of booze on the table and went in with the box of mulberries.

'Look at the young of today,' Daulatram's voice followed him. 'When they get a box, it is of mulberries. Not of sweets. Arre, whoever buys mulberries?'

Pushpa took the box and asked him, 'Tea? I am going to fry up some liver.'

Preparations seemed afoot for a nice party. When he had washed his face and come out, Bhikulal was saying, 'I thought I should get some for you to eat also before the season is over. I got payas. Have you seen them? Aren't they good! I roasted them at home. You can't roast them here. It will raise quite a stink.'

'By God, if it comes to roasting I can do a real good job. But these neighbours will arrive to complain. The stink will hang in for at least two days.'

'That is what. Now those days were different when we used to dhoono them. Mohallas were of the same community and nobody complained...'

'Why would anyone complain? They rushed in with big bowls, for the soup. Truly, you would run out of soup. It used to take three hours to cook. Now you will see, she will cook it within half an hour in the pressure cooker,' Daulatram was saying. He was very pleased.

Bhikulal was singing his own tune. 'So I got them roasted. Could get only six. Four of them are of the front foot. That too of the khassi goat.'

'I thought we could eat the liver to begin with. What is bahu doing? Doesn't take even ten minutes to fry liver...'

Adhirath picked up the bottle and screwed it open. When he began to pour three glasses, Daulatram turned to Bhikulal and said, 'This is today's youth. Will get drunk in the presence of their dads. How different it was when we were young. By God, we would take a sip or two hiding away from the elders. Truly, we dared not enter the house until Father had gone to sleep. We were scared that if he smelt booze on our breath, he would thrash us, right and proper.'

Bhikulal bent towards Adhirath and said, 'I forgot to tell you something. At least two men had been with her. Did the job, the whole thing with great gusto. She was full to the brim inside. Could also have been three.'

Pushpa came in with a plateful of sliced cucumbers, tomatoes and onions. In another plate she carried the fried liver, dark, almost black squares, triangles and other irregular pieces. Adhirath suddenly felt sick. He ran in.

'What was the matter?' asked Daulatram.

By the time Adhirath returned, Bhikulal had begun relating the whole story. He picked up his glass and went in. Scooping ginger and garlic paste from the grinder, Pushpa said, 'You went to see Mama? Never even told me.'

Adhirath came back to the outer room. He was sure Pushpa's ears must be fixed on their conversation. Today he did not hear the cooker being banged. She must have taken out the paraat. Must have kneaded the flour too. But it was all soundless. The half bottle was soon empty. Daulatram brought out a bottle from his own stock that was still more than half full. When he began to pour, Adhirath placed his palm on his glass silently refusing the refill.

'Arre, have some. Why are you feeling ashamed now?' Bapu shoved his hand aside and poured him a large drink.

He wasn't ashamed, the cucumber and tomatoes were boiling in his stomach, seeking more acid. He knew he would not be able to hold any more alcohol.

'Make the rotis thick,' Bhikulal stepped up to the doorframe in the room to tell his niece.

'No need to tell her that. If your niece had her way she would make a single roti of the whole dough.'

'Thick rotis are good to mop up the gravy,' Bhikulal was paying no attention to him.

'At what time did she die?' asked Adhirath.

'Dhattere ki, always talks of death,' Daulatram said and laughed.

'I have just talked to someone about Pushpa's promotion. You people sit around twiddling your thumbs. I know someone in the headquarters. Buddhan's son is posted there. The same Buddhan, my saali's dewar. He does the dusting there. He will talk to the sicetary of his union and will get him to recommend Pushpa strongly. You have to have someone to push the case. It has been over ten years, she must get promotion.'

'Fifteen...' Daulatram was now beginning to get truly drunk.

'Ten years since she came here.'

'Mamu, what time was the girl killed?'

'Between ten and twelve. At night. Dactor said so.' Now Bhikulal's tongue began to get slippery, 'Were you also involved, or what? Knew her?' He winked at Adhirath.

Adhirath stood up and went out. He climbed the stairs slowly. Varun must have already gone to sleep. When his father opened a bottle, Pushpa would send the boy upstairs with his grandmother to keep him out of harm's way. Upstairs he found both grandmother and grandson watching TV with full concentration. He fell on the bed and slipped into a comatose sleep.

4

Sunday. For others, a day to laze around. For him, another day of lazing around. Even so, he woke up late. Varun's place next to him was empty so even the boy was up and about. He saw a pile of washing lying on the floor, heard the grumbling of the washing machine competing with the noise from the road. Pushpa was doing her Sunday chores, her face sullen. She came in to sort out the washing to load the machine.

'Up?' she asked indifferently.

Yes, there are lucky blokes who go to sleep at night and never wake up and hitch a free ride on the shoulders of others to their final resting place. Adhirath was not so lucky. He had to get up to see a sulking wife. He fixed his gaze on her face. She was digging into the pockets of the trousers he had worn yesterday, and brought out things she did not expect to see. A broken piece of a turquoise bangle of thick glass, a handkerchief stained with mud, a small piece of sheer cloth with a frill of tiny beads, a torn end of a dupatta by the look of it, a receipt from the petrol pump, a golden button and some loose change. She placed the stuff on the corner of the bed and strode towards the washroom with an armload of soiled clothes. He pushed the stuff under the mattress and placing the button in his palm, gazed at it. It was definitely gold. And that glittering piece of something in its centre must be a diamond. He closed his fist and opened it to stare at it again. Was it a diamond? Must be worth at least a lakh. Or was it? Just how much do diamonds cost? However much, this diamond must be worth more. How much would that man pay to get it back?

'Whose trunk is that under the bed?' she asked. 'Nitesh gave it to you or what?'

Okay, so he had already told his bhabhi!

'Go ahead, tell him I have got it,' Adhir snapped.

'I don't tell anyone anything. I have learnt to keep my mouth shut.'

He kept quiet.

'When the government paid you to do all this, you complained all the time. Now you want to spend your own money to run here and there?' Pushpa was back in the room.

This aspect had not occurred to him.

'Will you get up? I got to put the sheet in the washing. Just think what mummy papa will say. Papaji has been fetching Varun from school every day. You are never around. And they take out their annoyance on me. The moment I enter the house I have to hear taunts about how much they are doing for me, for my child...and Varun is picking up foul language...'

He said nothing. Had he been the additional in-charge of his thana, this same woman, his wife, would not be so bothered about Varun learning some abuses. She would be roaming around the lane, her head held high with pride.

'So where have you been going?' she asked again.

He sat in sullen silence. Just because his earnings had dropped, had he lost the authority to make decisions and even his right to step out without informing anyone? Would they have dared ask him this a year ago when he was additional in-charge of a thana?

'You too have changed,' he said and went out onto the narrow landing from where the steps led down to his parent's part of the house.

When they got married, he had built this upper portion, one room, with a partition, like the one downstairs. One part for the cooking and washing, the other to sit and sleep in. Where was there to go? Across his house were those neighbours he could not stand. In the small open space between houses lay a pile of metal rods, rivets, strings and polythene bags. The very windows seemed to flap in despair at having nothing to take inside, not even a handful of clean, crisp air. All around him were neighbours, gargling, abusing, spitting and staring. On the road were cars and cycles and cycle rickshaws, vegetable vendors and the sound of people haggling for pennies.

He sat on the top step, buried his head into his knees and withdrew into himself.

He woke up with a start when Varun shook him. Amazing, he thought, you can shut out any amount of noise if you truly do not want to hear it. Is hearing not involuntary? Is it true? All those people who come to the police stations and claim they have not heard the screams of people being beaten to death; are they telling the truth? At least some of them?

'Papa, will you take me?'

He laughed.

What did the boy want? Where did he want to go? Varun looked confused. He saw his son's face pucker, and folding him to his chest, said, 'Of course I will take you. But you have to ask me once again, after you have given me a full-on kiss, okay?'

Varun planted a moist pair of lips on his cheek and told him. He wanted to go to the zoo. The tiger had had cute little cubs, he had just seen it on the news channel and grandpa wouldn't let him watch cartoons anyway.

That is how Pushpa found him, on the top step of the staircase, his child in his arms and both of them smiling.

'Go, get ready then,' he turned Varun away from the door towards the staircase and gave him a push. His mother could bathe and dress him.

Pushpa touched him on the shoulder and they went in. She began to fuss with the bed. He looked at her.

He came up behind her and hugged her close. She stopped pulling off the edges of the sheet from under the mattress.

'Should I change the sheet now or later?' she asked him raising an eyebrow meaningfully, a naughty question in her eyes.

He pushed her onto the bed.

She was smiling at him. 'Happy now?'

'I don't probably know what I am supposed to do. Always dissatisfied. Do you mind?' he asked hesitantly.

'Oh, no,' she said turning around in the circle of his arms and rubbing her cheek against his. Her eyes smiled into his. He laughed.

'Listen, you can tell Papaji you are doing your rounds to push for an early enquiry,' she said and squirming from underneath him, kissed him fully on the lips, then pinning his shoulders down, straddled him. Tracing the line of his jawbone from his ear to his chin with her index finger, she smiled radiantly at him. 'You do whatever you want to. Don't worry about anything. Not even money. I will provide for the house. Do what you want,' she said, her eyes shining with pleasure.

He jerked her off, got off the bed and walked out on her, banging the door behind him. She lay where she was, on the mattress with its sheet half tucked in. She pulled the sheet out from under the mattress viciously. The piece of broken-glass kangan under emerged to pinch her elbow. The loose coir threads in the mattress scratched her.

He came back after a while to grab the keys to his motorcycle. She was lying there on the crumpled bed, her eyes glazed.

'The best contraceptive in the world,' he said and walked out again.

'Am going to the zoo with the boy. You don't have to suffer my face anymore,' he screamed banging the door again.

Adhirath leaped down the stairs and heard his father lecturing his mother. 'Three apples are rotting. You think the money comes from your father's house that you can waste...'

At night he heard Pushpa's tears, falling softly on the pillow as she tightly pursed her lips trying to hold in her sobs.

Would he ever do anything right? He turned his back on her.

~

As he walked from the bus stop he could clearly see the house with the dome. No need for an address, the name of a street or the number of the house.

'Tell Saroj madam, the police is here,' he said to the guard sitting inside the open gate. The man stared at him suspiciously. 'Will you go or should I give you one?' he barked in a voice that left no doubt about his training as a cop. Without a uniform a man has no status, he thought. Had clothes been made to cover the body or be flags to advertise class and status?

This time Saroj met him under the dome. There were fewer stars on the ceiling of the dome. Curtains swayed to and fro as if dancing to some unheard music. She was in a salwar kurta. Black flowers were embroidered on the cuff of her white salwar and the black kurta had a long white yolk with black flowers embroidered on it. He had never seen such fine embroidery, the stitches almost feathery. She is truly a black and white film, thought Adhirath, and he recalled the yellow dupatta with its fringe of coloured beads.

'Listen, I don't have a search warrant but I thought I should see your bedroom once, if you have no objections...'

'Have to go somewhere. Meeting a friend. I was about to leave.'

'No problems,' said Adhirath. 'It will take only a minute.'

He fished out the button from his pocket and showed it to her. Saroj was not startled.

'Where did you find it? How much we looked for it on Holi. He even dropped the idea of wearing a kurta and put on a T shirt. I only told him that he could wear the kurta with one less button. The topmost button is always open, who will notice if that button hole has no stud? How does it matter? Even Papaji had to admonish him. That is when he agreed. Went and changed into a kurta. In this family it is the custom to wear new clothes and gold and silver ornaments. Without it, they don't play Holi.' A calm voice. No sign of any disturbance on her composed face. You can lie even without losing your poise.

'Had to ask you something,' Adhirath said. 'You said that your husband did not open the door even after loud and persistent knocking. You didn't call him on his mobile?'

'I did. Twice. I could hear it ring from outside the room. But he did not pick it up.'

Adhirath felt there was something wrong with her response. What was it?

'You didn't know that girl at all?'

'Who?' Saroj asked, her neck bent to one side.

What was the name of the girl? Adhirath was taken aback.

The girl with the yellow dupatta? She with the turquoise kangan? Pross? Randi? Beauty-parlour girl? Amirpurwali? The dead body in the farmhouse? How many ways to describe her and not one clue to her personality. She was called Suryabala, she chose to be Renu. When did names become part of one's identity? When there was no language, when people killed animals trapped in pits with rocks and tore them open to eat, did they have names then? When did they start giving names? In his son's text books, there were pictures of primitive people going about their work. They did not mention when names came into existence.

'The girl whose body was found in your farmhouse? You didn't know her name?' Adhirath said with a twisted smile, looking straight into her eyes.

'She said her name was Mohini. I didn't believe her.'

'Why?'

'They don't have such names in the villages. Mohini, Manisha, servants don't have such names. Had there been a film star of that name, I could have believed that the parents had named her that, but there is no film star by the name of Mohini.'

Adhirath shook his head. Names as indicators of status. Of caste. Of class. What a civilization human beings had evolved into.

'Why did she come here?'

'The driver brought her. Once. He said she was some distant relative of his and had done a beautician's course. He said she would do whatever was done in parlours, here at home. And if I liked her work, I could introduce her to the people I knew and she could build a clientele. I refused.'

'Why?'

Saroj looked at him as if he was a curiosity.

'I go to Claridges for my facials. Would I let this country

bumpkin touch me?' She set her head on one side in a gesture of contempt. 'Is it not enough that I have moved to this...' She bit her tongue.

'Moved to this...what?'

'Nothing.'

'Where are you from? Where is your parental house?'

'Civil Lines, it used to be there. Now it is in Panchsheel.' Saroj pressed a button on her mobile. 'I have to go. This button...' she let the words trail.

'Is it case property?' Adhirath completed the sentence for her.

She smiled again, slowly. That is when her mobile began to ring. She pressed a button and said very softly into it, 'Hello, my dear, just about to leave.'

A pause, then, 'Oh no!'

Setting the phone on the table, she said, 'My friend, whom I had to meet, can't make it. All of a sudden, some guests have arrived at her place. We have this horrible habit in our country of turning up, unannounced. Come, let me show you the bedroom.'

Adhirath now walked up the film-inspired wooden staircase with carved banisters. He found he could not touch them as he climbed to the first floor. The staircase ended in a bow-shaped landing with four doors opening out of it. Saroj turned left to the farthest door and went in. Adhirath had never tried to imagine the kind of bedrooms the rich would have but he could never have conceived of what he saw. He had expected grandeur and opulence, not the simplicity that faced him. No chandeliers, white ceiling with no gold leaf, wood floor, a simple bed with no carved headrest, stuffed armchairs with what looked like jute covers, no sculpture, no paintings. There were lamp shades of pale yellow paper. And yet it was beautiful. The deep green curtains swept down to the wooden floor, the red bedspread blazed in that quiet room, and accents of both the colours turned up in the facets of the crystal bowl set by the bedside with a single yellow flower floating in water. No door led outside other than the one through which they had come. The other door led to a dressing room with a walk-in wardrobe beyond which was a bathroom. There were durries on the bathroom floor and a vine climbed around the huge mirror. He touched the leaves. It was a real live plant, not a plastic creeper. He came back into the bedroom and moved the curtain. It covered a set of French windows that opened onto a balcony from where he could see the side of the house. He came in and shut the door, automatically bolting it, and noticed that the bolt was about a foot long, made of brass. A very old brass bolt. He looked around again and saw Saroj standing near the foot of the bed watching him.

'Over there, there is a way out, let me show you,' she said.

Adhirath was struck dumb. Saroj went out onto the landing and took him to the room at the other end from where a staircase led downstairs. The room was like a storehouse of games. A billiard table stood in the centre and against the walls were cricket bats, wickets, tennis racquets and such things. Tall boxes of cricket balls stood around, some open, some sealed. Adhirath looked at each bat longingly. If he could give Varun even one of these things he would come to believe his dad was a superman. His cricket bat was made of some cheap wood, not the obviously willow one here. He played cricket with plastic balls and stuck anything in the ground for stumps.

'Shall we leave?' asked Saroj.

Adhirath nodded.

'Today you have come alone. He didn't come with you? Your friend, the real policeman?' Saroj asked in her composed tone, as if making ordinary conversation. Adhir's eyes widened in surprise. Saroj's smile widened too.

'I am in the police too,' he said.

Saroj laughed, a simple polite laugh, not a derisive one.

'That button has yet not become case property,' Saroj said. 'I had guessed the very first time I saw you both.'

'Some policemen work in mufti, in plainclothes,' said an annoyed Adhirath.

'Daddyji does not pay attention to these things. He may not even have asked for your IDs. He is obsessed only with his astrologer and the avoidance of this colour or that food.'

Adhirath glanced back pointedly at the open bedroom door as he turned towards the stairs. Red bedspread. The father-in-law had been asked to avoid the colour red. Was that why the daughter-in-law was happily lolling on a red bedspread?

'I am not superstitious,' said Saroj and took the stairs down. Downstairs she said, 'I did not even offer you tea, Mister...?'

Adhirath told her his name.

'A very unusual name,' said Saroj. 'It is close to lunch time. Will you stay for lunch?'

'But you were going out somewhere,' he said.

'Yes, but it got cancelled, remember? I was not talking about my lunch, but about yours. I will only eat with my son, after fetching him from school. That is why I generally never fix a lunch appointment. Today I made an exception and see? It got cancelled. Now I won't go anywhere. So, will you have a bite?'

Adhirath refused. He had gone to Lakshmi Nagar after dropping his son to school and after roaming around for a while had had poori chole in a roadside shop. The pooris dripped oil. 'Do you fry them in Mobil oil?' he had screamed at the shopkeeper. He could still smell the strong spices of the chickpeas cooked in a hurry with the aid of baking soda. He was tempted to eat here, in their opulent drawing room. Might she seat him at the dining table? He wanted to see what the rich ate.

'No,' he said firmly. 'Must go. I too have to fetch my son from school.'

'Ok, let me drop you somewhere,' Saroj said. 'I have to go to DPS, Noida. I can leave a little earlier.' She went in and Adhirath sat down to count the stars twinkling under the dome.

'You have a lot of free time in your job. You can even go to bring your son home from school,' said Saroj as she drove her car out of the compound onto the road. 'Where should I drop you? Where do you live?'

'Mand...Madam, drop me at Lakshmi Nagar,' said Adhirath.

'So that button...'

'Do you want it?'

'Where did you find it?'

'Tell me if you want it,' he said.

'Will you give it to me?'

'No. Whether you believe it or not, it is case property. And I am in the police force.'

'It can become case property any time,' said Saroj. 'No, I don't want it.'

They were close to Lakshmi Nagar. Adhirath asked her to drop her at the red light. The car slid smoothly to a stop. He got down and turned, holding on to the door, 'I have heard that your farmhouse is to be sold.'

'I have heard this too,' said Saroj and smiled. She bent towards him and closed the door.

When Varun got home licking an ice cream, his grandmother was slamming the fridge door. 'Just look, from when is that dahi sitting here? It is covered with moss. This is how she throws money. Wastes everything. Why should she set so much yogurt? I don't even touch yogurt...'

Adhirath raised his eyebrows at Varun. 'Why, my darling son, will you eat some dahi?' Both laughed uproariously.

His dad came in holding on to his lungi with one hand and half a dozen bananas in the other. 'He gave it. Did I not say he is asking for ten rupees more...a government letter has arrived for you. Just see what it is.'

A brown envelope lay on the table that he had not noticed.

Adhirath opened it. It was the notice for the enquiry. He had to appear next Wednesday. He could bring his lawyer if he chose to for this was his right. He could make his statement or appoint a legal representative to do it. He felt his heart racing. He wished he had had his lunch at Saroj's place. Now he would not be able to eat a morsel.

When Pushpa returned home in the evening, she read the notice and quietly put on the saucepan for tea.

'He has been sitting there depressed ever since he saw it,' her mother-in-law said.

'He loses heart at the smallest thing. When you have a job like this you also have to have some guts. What was the need to join the police force if...' Daulatram began his usual harangue.

'So what else could I have done? Is it easy to get a job? How does it matter to you? You are the type who would say become a bus driver, or a conductor.'

'Listen to him! Have you heard what your darling son said...'

'Why are you bringing her in?' Adhirath suddenly exploded. 'How high your ambitions were for me I know! Look at the name you gave me. Adhirath. Wow, what a name, such a fantastic choice. What did you think, I would become the driver of a Mercedes?'

'Does anyone else have such a nice name? What is wrong with the name? It comes from the Mahabharat. He brought up Karna.'

'A driver, that is what he was...'

'He drove a rath. A carriage of the princes. Lord Krishna himself drove a rath. He became a saarathi.'

'What are you talking about at such a time?' his mother, Shakuntala Rani, said, coming to the outer room. She had got some mathri with pickles. Adhirath relished salt-less mathri with pickles. These, he saw, were salted. 'You don't even know how to boost his courage, arguing all the time.'

'Oh, come and pamper him, then,' Daulatram hit back. 'The sooner the matter is settled, the sooner he will get back to his job. What else will he learn now at home? Will he roll rotis? If you look at the way things are nowadays, that is all there is left for men to do,' he said, taunting his daughter-in-law who was entering with cups of tea on a tray. 'When women start wearing trousers, those who should wear trousers will knead flour...'

Ignoring him, Pushpa said, 'You should get a lawyer...'

'He will charge ten-twenty grand,' said Adhir spreading pickles on the mathri. 'Will see what happens.'

'You should have applied for an early hearing yourself. It has been nearly a year now. It had to happen someday. Once it is over, at least the matter will end.'

'I wanted it to keep getting delayed. They will find me guilty.'

'Not at all,' Pushpa said promptly. 'They have to protect their own. How can the department find you guilty?'

'We are in the department but we are not one of them. You know this as well as me. We will always remain outsiders. In fifteen years, I got one promotion. You got two. Does anyone have to wait so long for promotions? So don't talk rot.'

'With women, it is common,' she said. 'With me it is double discrimination. That is all right. I am quite happy to be where I am on the helpline. At least I have a shift duty. Now that I have a day shift I can at least get time to spend with my son.' She sipped at her tea. 'I say, engage a lawyer.'

'Can't you talk to someone? You too have bosses, officers, they can do something to help,' Shakuntala said.

'Arre, you think she will talk to someone...'

'That son of Buddhan's sister-in-law...'

'I don't know what rubbish you keep talking about. Which Buddhan?' Daulatram said contemptuously.

'How do I know? You were the one who said Buddhan's saali's son will talk...about bahu's pormotion.'

'Mummyji, leave it be. I am okay as an SI. If I become an inspector, I may be posted in a thana. Then I may have to work all the time, there will be neither day nor night for me.'

'Arre, Buddhan is her mamaji's saali's dewar. He is posted at the headquarters,' Daulatram said derisively. 'He is a peon, huh, who will listen to him...'

'Well, talk to him. Ask him to not try for bahu's promotion. To first get this enquiry settled in his favour.'

'Now you are making sense. I swear, for the first time in her life some sensible words have escaped your mother's lips. And why should they not? After all the matter concerns her darling son. Even otherwise it is not good for a woman's status to be equal to that of the man,' Daulatram said and placing his empty tea cup on the table, he said, 'Was there no milk?

Nowadays milk is so watery and nobody boils it for a long time to thicken it.'

'Enough,' Adhirath screamed all of a sudden. 'All the time you are thinking of food.'

Everyone got upset. All conversation stopped. After a while the TV began to talk.

'You call bahu's mamaji, I don't think he will do it,' Shakuntala said conspiratorially to her husband after the son and the daughter-in-law had gone upstairs.

In the room upstairs Shakuntala's son had fallen on the bed without having taken off his chappals. Covering him with a sheet, Pushpa was saying, 'The government's attitude has changed now. When I applied for a job, girls were not allowed to take the test for the ASI's position. They could enter the force only as constables. Now women can become ASIs right away just like men. Had I joined as an ASI I too would have been an inspector by now. I could have then been in a position to talk to someone.'

'Everyone is concerned only about herself,' Adhirath said, kicking his feet in the air. One of his chappals flew off angrily and hit the wall.

Two strangers lay down on the same bed, their backs to each other. There was such animosity here that even sleep was scared off and refused to enter the room.

5

'Yaar, that notice of the enquiry has come,'Adhirath told Nitesh. He had been sitting here for half an hour but Nitesh was busy preparing his reports. Each item had to be given a number, then noted in registers, there were dozens of such papers to prepare in a murder case.

'It has! Well, it had to come. How long would they put it off? Take my advice, just deny everything.'

'They are very clever people. It is not easy to make fools of them.'

'Who is doing it?'

'That Kashyap. He is a bastard of the first order. I have heard that ever since he has become a Deputy Police Commissioner, he doesn't care two hoots even for the Commissioner himself.'

For a while there was silence in the room.

'Yaar, if it was only a matter of losing the job it would not have mattered so much. I am afraid they may file a case against me.'

'Show me, show, what does the letter say?'

'Keep it. It is a photocopy,' said Adhir and took out three sheets of paper from his pocket. His hand brushed against the button.

Nitesh read the notice and began to shake his head.

'I have a friend, in the legal department. Was in college with me. Let us meet him.'

'We'll see,' said Adhirath and went silent.

'Did you get any more information on the case?' he asked after a while. He was in an acute dilemma about the evidence he had found. Should he hand all of it over?

'We thrashed that chowkidar well and proper. But I don't think he knows much. Just got the job. The old one is some Nachchatar Singh. Works at some farm close by. All of them were high. Says that day nobody came to the farm. He had seen the girl earlier, she came there four or five times. Kept visiting the place. That Nachchatar also said that the new chowkidar had been with him since noon. Nobody saw anything,' Nitesh said.

Adhirath put his hand in his pocket again and behaving as though he had recalled something he took out the piece of the kangan and the button and placed it on the table.

Nitesh's silence indicated that Adhirath had crossed some invisible line between the friendly and the professional. Suddenly Adhirath felt that he should not have trespassed onto his friend's turf. To accompany Nitesh was one thing; to go fishing for clues on his own was another. Nitesh could put a brake on his efforts whenever he wished.

'Sorry, yaar. I even went to meet her. Saroj. She says she does not know when the button was lost. It could not be found at home on the day of Holi.'

Nitesh stared at the button for a long while. There was an awkward silence in the room. At last Nitesh heaved a sigh.

'What would you have done had you been in my place?' Nitesh asked him straight. 'I will have to answer for this, na?'

'That is true. Listen, I am handing over whatever I found. I am not going to say I found these things.'

'So? Now whatever I found that day has been entered into the records. The file is ready,' Nitesh said. He picked up the button and began to rotate it. Every time the stone caught the light from a different angle it gave out a blinding glint. 'Is it a diamond?' he asked.

'Yaar please don't get offended. I know I should not have done this, it is your job. But since I had gone that side, I found this in the farm. I am under too much stress. This only helps me cope, that is all.'

'I found a lot of these pieces of glass,' said Nitesh suppressing his anger. 'But I did not find the diamond. Is there a witness that you found it there?'

'No,' said Adhirath. 'I worked alone.'

His face had fallen and his voice was low.

'There were many pieces of this bangle,' Nitesh said, staring at the turquoise piece of bangle and noticing Adhir's sad face, he added, 'Forget it, yaar, it does not matter. When there is a case pending against you, there is bound to be tension.'

'What was the name of that girl?' asked Adhirath.

'Basanti. That is what she told Udairaj. I say her mother may have truly liked *Sholay*, what! But here she was known as Renu. And later we found out that her mother had given her some other name. Something else it was. Can't recall. She was very pretty. Shall I show you her photo?'

Adhirath prevented himself from saying 'Suryabala'. He no longer dared tell his friend that he had met her mother.

Nitesh opened a file and placed a picture before him. It was a close-up only of the face. Closed eyes. She did not look dead. She did not even look very pretty in the photograph. Sometimes very good-looking people begin to look ordinary printed on paper. Suryabala. Basanti. Mohini. Renu. Was she truly a prostitute? At least he had seen the face of the person for whom he had taken on such a headache. But then was he doing all this for her? Or for himself?

'Was she tall?'

'Smaller even than medium height. You can't tell from the photograph but she was very beautiful. Chowkidar said the pradhan had his eyes on her. Whenever a car came to the farm the pradhan would start hovering around. He and that former sarpanch. Seems both the oldies have nothing else to do. If you believe the chowkidar they are always strolling on the road. Or they sit on the roadside on a cot. No girl dares come late from school.'

'They must definitely know something,' said Adhirath.

'That is true. I spoke to both of them. They denied everything. They knew the girl, only this much they admitted. The pradhan said she was like his granddaughter, her character was bad. Once he had even sent a man to her house to warn her mother and to tell her that her daughter had strayed onto a very bad path and she should make her correct her ways. Once both the old fogies had caught hold of her and asked her to come home the next day. They claim that they wanted their wives to talk to her and make her mend her ways. She did not go to meet them,' Nitesh laughed loudly.

'Wanted to give her advice? Those bastards have ants in their pants!'

'I'm going to the village again today. Come with me. Looks like your investigation is progressing better than mine.' Nitesh could not stay angry with his friend for long.

Adhirath shook his head. 'Yaar, if I go on my own, I might get some stuff for you. Do me a favour. Let me work on this case for a bit. I have too much tension now. It will divert my attention.

When the case is solved, you get yourself photographed with the murderer.'

He placed two bottles of chilled beer in front of Bharat. He had bought them from the liquor vendor in the village. The shop had both country liquor and that strangely named breed, Indian Made Foreign Liquor. For the first time he had inspected the little market closely. Even in such a small place there were two shops selling meat! Four sold laddoos. One 'doodh, dahi, caream, desi ghee and makhan' shop. Then there were shops selling agricultural implements, light bulbs and plastic ware. There was also a '*Sunny Hair Stylist*' and on the platform outside it, sat the pradhan.

The pradhan had recognized him, 'Why sir, making many rounds of the place I see?'

'Looking for land,' Adhirath said and before the conversation could proceed said Ram Ram and escaped. This, he could see, was the dictator of the village.

'Pradhanji is sitting at the hair ishtylisht's,' he said taking out the opener from his pocket and popping the bottles open.

'That is the only thing he does. Pradhan once, Pradhan forever. That shop is actually his. He has rented it out. Used to be a big zameendaar, now he may have about three acres. Sold all the rest.'

'You have zamindars even now?' asked Adhirath surprised.

'Not that way. Whoever has zameen is zameendaar. About ten people had a lot of land in the village. The rest are workers. They grow something on shamilat land. You know land around the village is counted as a part of the village and it is known as shamilat. They work as farm labour. Or do some other work. Work in the village ischool.'

'Did you find out about the land for me?' Adhirath asked, holding on to his excuse for interest in the area.

'Had you told me earlier, I would have got some radishes,' said Bharat after a swig and a burp. 'Drinking on empty stomach can give you gas. Beer has a lot of gas. That is why the lid pops open like this. Did you see how it flew off?'

'Get those radishes then. I will get two more bottles,' said Adhirath. He was enjoying himself now. Pushpa had even packed four rotis for him. Who knows whether Bharat had got something to eat or not. His scooter was parked close by.

'I have rotis,' said Adhirath.

'That I also have got from home. Will eat later.' Bharat took out a fifty-rupee note from his pocket. 'This time my treat.'

Adhirath refused to take the money.

'Next time, the booze will be mine,' Bharat promised. 'And wild hare.'

A Honda City passed with Pradhanji on the back seat. Bharat raised his hand and said Ram Ram loudly.

'I feel so good here,' said Adhirath lying on the cot. Two beers, two radishes, pickles, aalu-baingan ki sabzi and rotis had made his stomach heavy and his heart light. Bharat stretched out on a sheet he had spread on the pile of bricks. When they woke up, the sun was about to set. Had he come here to get some rest? How all the tension had vanished. He had forgotten everything, his office, the pending enquiry. Had Nitesh come this way today? Had he seen them snoring away? He began to get tense again.

'What will I tell the boss?' asked Adhirath waking up to his assumed identity. 'Must leave now. Takes a long while to get back. Today it took me three hours to get here.'

'My ancestors were in the army of Surajmal Jat. Tales of

those times are recounted in the family. It is said that if they left in the morning they reached Delhi in the evening.'

'Did they walk?'

'On horses. They would not have made it in one day if they walked.'

'Nowadays we have horse power!' said Adhirath patting his motorcycle. 'This animal never tires. Even then it takes so much time.'

'That faramhouse you were asking about? More than half of the land is in the name of the daughter-in-law. Some part is in the name of the son. So actually there are two registries. If they want they can sell half also. I don't know who owns the strip that gives them access to the entire plot. Meaning the pathway that leads to the house. If it is registered as a joint property with the buyer of half of the land then the problem of access can be solved. We can calculate the value and the buyer can pay half of the value and get his name added to the ownership deed. It can be done. There is no legal obstacle. But both the parties have to agree. I will have to ask them. If you give me the go ahead I will.'

Adhirath was looking at Bharat's face. A broad face that looked like it was made of sand. The simple face of a simple man. But could he be trusted? Was his face a real indicator of his personality? He might even be clever for all Adhirath knew. One has to be a little crooked to be a property dealer. He might have learnt some tricks of the trade too but he looked like a simple honest man who said what he felt. In only two meetings he felt he had come to get to know him well. Adhir felt bad at pulling the wool over his eyes. Both of them left together.

Near the station, Adhirath stopped next to a small pothole as if his motorbike had some trouble crossing it and stood to one side holding it. Bharat turned his scooter towards the village.

When he saw the scooter vanish, he turned towards the Bindal farm. The gate opening onto the narrow pathway was as usual closed. He inserted his hand through the gap in the iron grille. It was bolted and locked. He shook the gate forcefully. 'Open up' he shouted. At last, a man emerged from somewhere behind the house and limped towards the gate. 'Who is it?' he asked as he neared the gate.

'I have come to see the farm. It is for sale, isn't it? I am planning to buy it. Want to see it from inside.'

'No orders to show it,' said the man.

'Do you have orders to allow the pradhan in? You are Chetilal, aren't you?'

'No, sahib, nobody entered.'

'Open,' barked Adhirath in his cop voice.

'Will get the keys,' said the man turning back towards the house.

Fishing out the mobile from his pocket, Adhirath put it to his ear and said, 'Oye, come here, listen to this.'

'Who is it?' Chetilal turned towards him.

'The driver. He says you were here only that night, the night of the murder,' he said pressing a key on the keypad. The mobile lit up. Chetilal pushed his hand through the grille and took the mobile with a trembling hand and put it to his ear. He kept helloing into it but got no response for there wasn't anybody at the other end. Adhirath took his phone back and said, 'Looks like he disconnected. He said that you did it, that murder. Must have got scared of you.'

This time Chetilal took a set of keys from his pocket and opened the gate. Following him to the verandah of the house Adhir said, 'Listen, Chetilal, I am not the police. I have some other work here. My employer wants to buy this property. If he is about to buy, he will also seek some information. There has been a murder here. Now tell me the truth. What happened that day? Do the villagers invite outsiders like you to come paint their wives' faces with gulaal? If you tell me any lies, I will break your other leg also.'

Chetilal collapsed on the floor and began to hit his forehead with his hand. He rued the day he had allowed his uncle to talk him into taking the job here. 'I managed on half a roti where I was earlier. And where is the ghee on my roti here? My chacha works at the manure farm at Amirpur, just behind this farm. I used to carry headloads of dung there. Only two months ago, chacha became a caretaker here and got me to work as a helper. Nachchatar used to work here then, but he quit the job. Last month even the manager left. Then my chahcha also stopped working here. Who was left? Chetilal. I had to cut the mustard myself. Three days of work. So much work to do. Then cook your own roti after labouring the whole day in the sun. Electricity only at night and that comes and goes. At night, water the plants. Never mind the snakes. Oh yes, snakes. Long vicious ones. The poor have nothing but problems. Now the police come to thrash me. I am paying for the sins of some kullachini.'

Another name for Suryabala, thought Adhirath, a name signifying a woman of bad character.

'She came often, did she?'

'Three, no may be four times since I started working here. With Chhote Maalik.'

'Who is Chhote Maalik? Udairaj?'

'Yes. That deeraaiver would bring them. At night. Always at night. Once he spent two days here.'

'Deeraaiver, that driver? Would he also stay or leave after dropping them?' Adhirath's heart began to race.

'He stayed. He would sleep on the cot outside my room. Or on my cot. I would spread a durree on the floor. Nobody cares for the poor,' Chetilal sighed.

'What did you say the name of the girl was?'

'How would I know her name? Was she going to tell me her name? Such an arrogant thing!'

'When was the last time she came here?'

'Must have been a month. I was preparing to cut the mustard. That is when they stayed for two days. The manager used to come in the morning. To him she said...here, right here on the verandah where you are sitting, she sat here and said to him, she would buy a faram nearby. She asked him, "Will you manage my faram also?"'

'Really?'

'Yes. I was watering this climber. That is how I heard this. So much bapka! Giving orders like she owned the place. Get me this. Or that. Those days there used to be a lot of vegetables here. jhukni, brockli. I had never seen such vegetables in my village. Chhote Maalik left only after sacking the manager. He never came this side again. Since then, I am alone here.'

'Where does the manager live?'

'Sahib, his fate was even worse than mine. His daughter had had a daughter. He was going to do her chochak, you know, the ritual you have to do when your daughter becomes a mother? The tirain had an accident and he died in it. On the spot.'

'That train, the one that was going to Gorakhpur and had an accident? He was on that train?'

'Yes, yes. That one,' Chetilal said.

'What happened on the day of Holi? Did they come here?'

'No, sahib. Nobody came the whole day. I just went and got the people on the nearby farams to put a tika on my head.'

Now Chetilal began to cry in earnest. 'A day of tevhaar, a festival. Everything so quiet. Late afternoon, I went to Nachchatar's place. When I got there, I saw they had opened a bottle. I also gave twenty rupees. Nachchatar's son went on his cycle and got another bottle from the village. Everybody got nicely drunk.' Chetilal said he slept at Nachchatar's place and he also had the 'permisan' of the maalik so he felt free to do as he chose.

'You had permisan?'

'I called Chhote Maalik from Nachchatar's phone. I asked him. Only then I stayed there. He said, very well, enjoy your Holi.'

By the time Adhirath made Chetilal go with him on his bike to Nachahtar's farm, it was dark. Lights began to wake up here and there. The birds protested the departure of day, their calling reaching a crescendo and then falling into silence. He heard the sound of hooves. 'Neelgai,' said Chetilal. He could not see the animal but now the ride felt like a walk in the forest. He thought he could ask Cheti to lend him his cot.

Nachchatar lived on a farm with several rooms in a row that were rented out. He was now a small-time labour contractor, but sometimes advised Cheti about work at the Bindal farm too.

Nachchatar was cooking dinner and confirmed whatever Cheti had told them. He was not prepared to say anything more although Adhirath asked him about his bosses and their ways.

'They are nice people,' was all that Adhir got out of him.

'Then why did you quit?'

'I am old now. I can't work so hard,' he said and began to poke at the contents of the utensil on the stove with a long-handled spoon.

Four or five people gathered to listen. Some picked their teeth; some nodded their heads sagely. They began to add to the story. Adhirath gathered that all of them had been there on Holi. Fires began to be lit in chulhas outside the doors of the rooms and the aroma of frying spices began to fill the air. If you roasted knuckle bones here, would the smell of burning hair hang in the air or would it be dispersed far by the breeze? Perhaps it would spread all over and people would start running to them with bowls for the soup. How peaceful it was. 'Hutt,' he heard a voice that sounded like 'get lost' in Hindi. He looked up startled.

'It is an owl,' Nachchatar said. 'Lives here.'

The owl was right. This peace he knew now was only the absence of noise. There had been a murder here. There could be another. Adhirath began to make a move to leave. He peered outside the circle of light that the lamp in Nachahatar's room threw. It was dark for the moon was waning. Chetilal got up with him.

'Go only by the main road, sahib,' Nachchatar said. 'Sometimes you meet snakes on the kutcha road.'

'Arre, he has a motorcycle so he will take the main road only,' said Cheti.

'Tell me, why did you not tell the police all this?'

'They never asked, sahib. They only asked me when I had quit my job and what time Cheti came here that day. Anyway, why should we tell the police anything?'

When he dropped Cheti at the Bindal farm he did not feel like leaving the place at all. He switched off the engine and began to walk slowly with the bike by his side. It gave him a few more minutes in this peaceful place. Chetilal had shut the gate. The bolt was in, the lock in its place. The road was empty and quiet. If someone came here now, who would notice? Who knows who had come here that night? Had a car come, someone would have seen the headlights.

All of a sudden, he heard footsteps behind him like someone was chasing him. The blood froze in his feet. He could not move at all. Then he heard a sort of faint whine like the one that children make when they are unable to decide whether to bawl or not. He got onto his bike in a hurry. The illusion of peace had been shattered. It would be best to run away. That is when he heard the call 'Sahib, sahib...'

He turned. It was Chetilal.

'What is it?' he asked harshly.

'That Parduman, he...'and his teeth began to chatter.

'Hurry up. Parduman, what?'

'I am going to Nachhatar's. I will sleep there.'

'I will throttle you now. Has Parduman done something that you are so frightened? There is something you know that you are not telling.'

Chetilal sat down on the road. Adhirath kick started his bike and sped up to the gate of the farm. The gate was open. He went in and looked around. A person could hide anywhere among the trees and their shadows. Even at the back of the plot, trees stood still like guards. He banged on the door of the house. It was closed from inside. There was no movement inside. When he got out, Chetilal was standing in the middle of road shaking like a leaf in a strong wind.

'Now tell me. Has the driver come here for the first time that you are pissing in your pants?'

'He was standing here sahib, near the gate behind the tree. Why would he need to hide? I was about to go to my room having locked the place. I saw him. The car is not here. What is he doing here? What does this mean, sahib?'

He got Cheti to sit pillion and drove him to Nachchatar's room. When he turned to drive back, he found Bharat's scooter following him. He had to stop.

'Did you go to check with Nachchatar about the faram? Yes, it is fertile. They have water also. Lots of it and it is sweet,' said Bharat. 'So now you will check with your employer, will you? Get them here once, they will see it for themselves. That is when I will talk to the faramhouse people.'

Adhirath felt that Bharat had guessed everything so there was hardly any need to hide anything from him now. Even otherwise, how can anyone hide anything in a village?

'I want to tell you something.'

'Hoon,' said Bharat.

'I am not looking for any land. I am a cop.'

'I guessed that very day. But you are doing no work. Looks like you are enjoying friendship with me, na?'

'It's very tough to get the villagers to tell you anything,' Adhirath said. 'You say nothing remains hidden in a village. Here whoever I talk to claims that he knows nothing.'

'Silence can treat a hundred diseases,' Bharat said. 'Now look at me. You bid me goodbye and did not leave. I left but I got to know where you went, who you talked to and what you talked about. Everything. In a village you can only survive if you keep your mouth shut. Suppose the pradhan is doing something and you see it. You have to pretend you saw nothing. Everyone carries a needle and thread to stitch their lips shut. After all the panchayat is his, na?'

'Then tell me, a woman was killed in the farmhouse, nobody went into the farmhouse. How did it happen?'

'Maybe a ghost did it!' said Bharat and began to giggle.

Adhirath said nothing. Sure, blame a ghost. It was not his headache. Whoever did it, how did it matter to him? Now he had told this man too who he was. He wasn't even drunk. Anyway, how drunk can you get on two beers and that too after a nap? He had no excuse to justify such carelessness. Then he recalled how rested he had felt after such a long time. That is why he might have felt so generous, even grateful to Bharat. He had begun to feel that the world was not such a bad place after all. Anyway, what was done could not be undone. He should leave now.

'Come tomorrow evening. You will get to talk to everyone. But don't tell anyone about your being in the police. Nobody opens his mouth in front of the police, believe me.' What choice did Adhirath have but to agree? 'You haven't already told them, have you? Does not matter even if you did. I will handle them all. Anything else?'

'I haven't, but you don't go telling everyone. After all you are a villager, you will be on their side.'

'I am not from this village,' said Bharat.

Adhirath kept quiet.

'What are you thinking?' Bharat asked.

'I was thinking, there will be rabbit, and booze, if there were something else too...'

'Oh, something else to enjoy? Or should I say "someone"? Unluckily she has been killed or I would have checked,' Bharat said and began to laugh.

'You had asked her earlier? For someone else?'

'I don't get involved in such things. But that pradhan, I have heard that he and the former sarpanch, both of them had had a dip. On the night of Holi. Sunny had gone to massage the pradhan and saw this big mark on his shoulder. As if someone had bitten him. There were scratch marks also. But the real information is this. That night they were both missing for quite some time. When they returned they looked very calm and cool. You understand? As if some itch had left them. Everybody is talking. That the girl has left a mark of love on him. Love bite. You understand?'

Adhirath understood.

When Adhirath went to fetch his son from school on his motorcycle, Varun was thrilled to see him. He kept asking his father to stop along the way, calling out to his mates by name. Adhirath was nearly moved to tears.

'Have you now shown everyone that you are riding home on a bike?' he said lifting the child on to the pillion. 'Will you have almond milk?'

He drove to a nearby milk and paneer booth and bought a bottle of milk for the child. Having dropped him outside the house, he sped away. Now it was beginning to get warm. His hair felt matted inside the helmet. He began to sweat. The perspiration did not run in a rivulet down his cheek but lingered as a dampness on his skin. The moment he reached the village road, he took off his helmet. Who cares for rules in a village? Come to think of it, who cares for such things even in the city? Had someone even stopped him, he would have told them that he was in the force.

From a distance he saw some men running with lathis in their hands. Bharat was screaming something at them. He ran to his motorcycle when it stopped and said, 'You have come at a good time. Watch the hunt. Ten-eleven are already in the bag.'

Adhirath noticed then that knives were tied to the lathis. Bharat picked up a pebble and threw it at a big bush of jhund. A grey hare leapt out and ran towards Bharat, paused and turned back at high speed, and ran straight towards the hunters poised with their crude spears. The lathi swung in the air and tracing a trajectory like a javelin sailed towards the hare and rammed into the neck of the animal. The stricken animal kept running, propelled by its own momentum, the javelin sticking out of its throat, before it fell and flopped around, heaving in death. This is how people must have hunted in days gone by, thought Adhirath, and now this has become the javelin throw, an Olympic sport. Adhirath had also thrown javelins in school. He had not thought of it as a homage to the primitive hunter.

'All preparations have been made for the party,' said Bharat. The hunter picked up the limp body of the animal, pulled it off the spear and stuffed it into a loose cloth bag, hanging from his shoulder and moved on to look for more prey.

'You recognized him, didn't you?' said Bharat to Adhir. 'It is Nachchatar. He is a very good hunter. He is the one who hunts them for the pradhan. We have got permisan from the pardhan. The animals belong to those to whom the village belongs, na? Only villagers can hunt in their own territory. Whatever we kill today, we have to give a part to the pradhan. And a bottle too. Shall we go to the booze shop?'

Then noticing Adhirath's expression he asked, 'Are you feeling sick?'

Adhirath tried to laugh. 'Left early in the morning. Ate a filthy bhatura.'

Bharat nodded in agreement. 'The oil now is no longer pure, not even in the village.'

One man had accepted another man's excuse for his weakness and allowed his claim to manhood to stand. What else is friendship?

The booze shop owner was dozing outside his shop.

'Why Sethji, feeling sleepy?' Bharat asked him. Then turning to Adhirath he said, 'Munnalal opens the shop at six in the morning. And he's here till ten at night. Aren't you?'

'Till eight,' the booze shop owner stood up. 'Hunting is on I see. Struck some deal for a plot?'

'No deal,' said Bharat. 'Market is down nowadays. When the price of land goes up, the number of buyers goes down. But I have made a new friend. Who knows, he may get me a buyer.' He introduced Adhirath to Munnalal. 'Thought I would throw him a proper village party. You can still digest a rabbit now. Soon it will be too hot to digest it. In the summers, rabbits are hot food.'

'Last year Tillu ate rabbit in the summer,' said Munnalal. 'What a nosebleed, just wouldn't stop. Tillu's mother says to me, "Shut the shop, it is a sin, selling booze, and the sin is visiting our son." You may want a full bottle today.'

'Give one of rum. If we need anything later, we can get it later. On special days you do keep it open till nine or ten, na? In the city shops remain open till eleven.'

'Eight o'clock. After that Tillu comes to harass me...' Munnalal said entering his shop.

'Arre, what are you saying. On the day of Holi it was open for so long...'

'I had downed the shutter,' Munnalal said, 'Now you know if Pardhanji comes you may have to even break open the lock if necessary. That too because he is not even our Pardhanji. He is the pradhan of the neighbouring village so double burden, one he is a pradhan, on top of that, he is a guest.'

'That day Pardhanji had a lot to drink. Told me. Now I have to give him a bottle, will give the same one, which one was it?'

'Bhisky. That too Gilby.'

'Oh my, I shouldn't have asked. It means getting someone to loot my pocket,' said Bharat putting his hand in his pocket. 'Ok, give that Gilby. And one rum.'

Adhirath began to feel guilty watching him blow up so much money but he was in no position to share the expenses. Even so he took out his wallet.

'Put it away. You can get robbed even here nowadays,' Bharat said. 'I hope Pardhanji does not come at night for another bottle. I can afford only this one.'

As they passed by Sunny Hair Stylist shop Bharat called to the owner loudly, 'How are you Sunny? All well? Do some styling of my friend's hair too. Look at him, how he is growing his hair, like some girl. Come over to Nachchatar's.'

The bottles would not fit in the box attached to the motorcycle so Bharat held the bag with the bottles between Adhirath's back and his abdomen and said, leaning close to Adhir, 'That day Pardhanji must have taken this very road. After nine at night. Must not have been alone. That former sarpanch. They are always together. Like twins.'

Getting off the bike, Adhirath asked him, 'Why? Don't they have a car?'

'They do. But it is like this, an old man can't learn to ride a horse, na? Just look what an important thing I have said. The boys may have already passed out.'

Adhirath swallowed the information. But this was only salt. The meat was served only at night.

A man was grinding garlic and chillies on a grinding stone. Sticks piled in a makeshift stove of bricks were being lit. The hares had been skinned and chopped, and the pieces were heaped on a tray, the skins missing. Adhirath walked away to stroll in the fields and soon Bharat came to call him. 'Feeling good? Pure air, pure water. But you have work to do.' Adhirath burst out laughing. He wasn't on duty. He had no duty. And even if he had promised Ramwati, he could always find out from Nitesh and tell her something.

When the booze began to flow, tongues began to wag. At first, he and Bharat were served drinks in glasses. Both of them sat on a cot. The farm on which Nachchatar rented one of the row of rooms was a small one, and all the tenants gathered around them. There were some others too. All of them were talking.

'Arre, Nachchatar, how are you making do here? Happy?' asked Bharat. 'There you had so much fun.'

'What to do sahib, one has to make do,' said Nachchatar.

'His employer is going to buy. Nachchatar knows everything. Tell him what grows well there.'

'Yes,' said Nachchatar. 'That is what he said. He came here yesterday.'

'Madam did not ask you to come work for her again?'

'No. I have heard that she hasn't been to the farm in a year or so.'

It was odd, listening to them talk, to see how these men, who worked on such large fields where you could hardly hear when another person called out, who would not be allowed to listen to the conversations of their employers at any time, and who had never seen the houses of the farmhouse owners in the city, knew such a lot about them.

Nachchatar had worked for the Bindals from the day they had bought the farmland. The whole plot was 17.3 acres, he said. Of these, nine acres had been registered in the name of Bahuji. Her parents had paid for the land. The day the land was registered, that day in the registrar's office the Vaseeka Navees...

'Who is this Vaseeka?'

That led to a lot of laughter. Bharat told him that the, 'deed writer is known as vaseeka navees. He is the one who knows what the government rate of land is and how much stamp duty you have to pay.'

'Vaseeka Navees knew my father,' Nachchatar said.

He had got him the job on the farm. Bapu, he said, used to serve tea at the court. By caste they were maalis. He knew everything—making beds, planting nurseries, weeding, manuring. But he had to admit that Madam also knew a lot of gardening. She could wield the spade as well as any gardener. She had made so many different kinds of foreign flowers bloom in her garden. When the house was built, she handpicked everything. In the beginning she used to come to the farm regularly. Used to say that when the house is built she would move in, live here. Then the house was completed but by then she had had her child. She never stayed here but all the trees on the farm were planted by her. She used to do everything with enthusiasm and care. Everyone grows mustard and wheat but she grew barley, oats, foreign varieties of corn and even baby corn and many different kinds of vegetables that he had never seen before.

'Baby coran, you know, you have a special technique to grow it. Madam taught me. When the male flower forms, each and every flower has to be plucked. Before it blooms. I did not even know that there is a male flower in the plant. If you don't pluck the flower what happens is that the cob begins to form seed. Then it does not remain soft. It must not be fertilized, that is what she told me. Once she said that she would grow rice on a small plot. I said this soil is sandy, it will not hold water. So she told me there is no need to fill up the plot with water. You can grow rice without water logging also. It will need irrigation, that is all. She got some special seed. The plants also came up but they got burnt in the sun pretty soon, in a couple of days.'

Everyone laughed. Someone remarked that nobody can grow everything; just because you have money does not mean you can grow whatever you want to.

'Okay, okay. Tell us what happened on the day of Holi,' said Bharat.

'What is there to say? When Bahuji stopped coming, I quit the job. Now if something goes wrong with the tractor, there is nobody to get it repaired. This year they harvested mustard on only four acres and that too with great difficulty. For nearly a year and a half, only Maalik would come here. Bahuji would not set foot here. Earlier that deeraaiver, Parduman, he would come to enjoy himself. He brought seed, he would take back vegetables. Get the house cleaned. He had the keys to the house. Sometimes he spent the night here. Then he began to get that girl. My life became hell. We are not such people. Once I called Bahuji and Chhote Maalik picked up the phone. I told him what was happening. He said he would come here and teach Parduman the lesson he deserved. Asked me to call him the day he brought the girl. I called him the next time the fellow came. Chhote Maalik reached the place that very day. After that so much filth was spread that I cannot even begin to describe it. Don't even ask me.'

'What happened?' Adhirath felt the blood race in his veins.

'I left the job, sahib. We are decent folks. I also have a wife, back in my ancestral village. I left and never went back. Bahuji asked me many times to come, but I did not go. It has been over a year now. They kept getting people to look after the place for short periods. Then Cheti started working for them. And look the police has broken his leg. I swear by my mother, sahib, we never do anything dirty. Where there are dirty goings on, I won't live there. I know this man; he is very decent. He will not steal a guava. I should have got the poor lad to quit too when there was time.'

'This thing happened on Holi. I have been wondering how

it happened. Nobody came. Nobody stayed at the faram and look, they found the body of that woman there. I wonder what happened,' said Bharat almost as if to himself. Adhirath could tell he was fishing for more information. Sunny arrived and created a welcome disruption. He settled on the charpoy with Adhirath and Bharat.

There was a pause and plates were replenished, glasses refilled. Adhirath felt that nobody wanted to talk about that day. They seemed to think that if they so much as mentioned that day something worse could happen. They all began to talk about other things. When they were all a little high, Bharat returned to that day.

'What ill omen happened that day that you can't even talk about it? Here I was thinking that we are all friends here, we are like family. We are not going to tell anyone. One just wants to know what the mystery is. If the police came here and gave you two kicks you would all be babbling all night. And forgetting all about omens,' Bharat said.

Nachchatar started talking about it. 'Everyone had done their tika in the day only. This Cheti came here at noon. There were others too. We had some bhang. I won't lie sahib, it is evening time and lights are on. God is watching. The bhang grows here, wild. We plucked it and ground it and made our drinks. We do it off and on.'

'I have heard...' began a man and suddenly went silent. Bharat asked him to elaborate, many times.

'Arre, what he will hear, mad man,' said Nachchatar cautioning him to silence.

'Don't stop him. He will forget whatever he knows, for sure. Here I am thinking these are my own people and getting booze for you and you are treating me like I am an outsider. Hiding things from me. I am an outsider and so are you. We should be all united or not?' Bharat's tone was miffed.

'That former sarpanch, he came to get a haircut. He said his Holi had been fantastic. He was saying that night something did happen in the Bindal faram. They were passing by and saw something. He said there was no car there but the lights were on,' Sunny said.

'That is what I heard,' said the man who had begun it all. 'That former sarpanch, I have heard, went to a doctor to get his hand bandaged, here,' he placed his hand on at the base of the little finger of his left hand. 'He said that the night of Holi he was giving a bone to a dog and the dog bit him. But he did not get injection for dog bite. I told him he should get those injections, the fourteen injections they give you when a dog bites you. It is very dangerous, this kind of deep bite. He began to scold me. Said you mind your own bijness. People, you know, were saying...'

'What?' asked Adhirath despite himself.

'Arre, say it,' said Sunny. 'Let me tell you. In the village they are saying, it was not a dog but a bitch that bit him. A wild bitch!' he winked as he said this. Everyone began to laugh.

'He said that the lights were on in the farm? Then?' Adhirath wanted to take the conversation back to the half-told tale of that night. His glass sat in his hand, untouched.

'I said you should have gone in. You have been the sarpanch, who can dare not let you in? He says, I went. That deeraaiver was there. He had brought that girl with him. He said he threatened to call the police. He told the deeraaiver he can't run a brothel in the village.'

'Is that all? He just threatened and came away?' Bharat said. 'Is that how a leader should behave?'

'He told me that he wanted to call the police the next day but the police came on its own. The randi was also taught the lesson she deserved.'

'This sarpanch has become decent, has he? And that pardhan? They must have been together. They simply issued a threat and came away? Why did they not call the police?'

'Sahib, do these faram people also vote in elections of the panchayat?' Cheti asked him.

'Listen to him, now! How are they concerned with matters of the village?' Nachchatar said. 'They are big people. Work in the city. That is why village people let us stay here because we work for them, we have their backing. Otherwise they would have swallowed us alive by now. That is why nobody gets their bahu-beti here.'

Nachchatar said that when her child was small, Saroj Madam used to get him to the farm. He used to run a lot in the field. Open fields. No fear of any traffic. He climbed trees. She had also slung some swings made of ropes, some long swings also in which people could go to sleep.

'They call them something. She had told me. Yes, hemok. After that she began to send seeds with Parduman. He took back vegetables. The munnayger arranged for everything that needed to be done. After that even the munnayger lost his job. Then he lost his life.'

'After that the deeraaiver became so daring, I can't tell you,' said Cheti. 'And that woman too. Earlier she used to stay with the Maalik at night and sometimes the deeraaiver brought her here in the day. She began to think she owned the place. And that Chhote Maalik would dance to any tune she played.'

'Was the maalik going to marry her?' asked a man.

'What rubbish you talk,' Nachchatar snapped. He sounded

as if the man who had suggested this had insulted him. 'Who ever marries a whore? She first passed from under the deeraaiver's thighs. She was asking for money. That is all.'

Nitesh arrived to pick up Adhir and said, 'I told that Dalchand we will meet him in the court.' This was big of Nitesh because Adhirath's house was not on his way. From Lakshmi Nagar he had to turn towards Mother Dairy and had to go to Mandawali and then retrace his steps to get to Karkardooma Court. He drove steadily on, ignoring Adhir's advice that there was another way through Patparganj.

Adhirath was sure that if Nitesh had not asked Dalchand, he would definitely not have come to the court. Perhaps Adhir himself would not have gone. He did not feel like talking about his case. He was going through a phase in which he felt that if he did not think or talk about something, that thing would vanish. And he wanted certain things to remain invisible for as long as possible.

The lawyer had asked them to come only after four in the afternoon. The Karkardooma Court was still quite crowded. The new court building had begun to look old and faded already. The walls were splattered with paan stains. Cigarette boxes, wrappers, empty pouches of paan masala and polythene bags covered the grounds, the stairs and the floors.

When they reached the room of the lawyer he wasn't there. His munshi recognized Dalchand and offered them chairs and gave them tepid water to drink. He told them that the lawyer was in another lawyer's chamber, discussing some case.

By the time Ashok Verma, MA, LLB arrived in his chambers, Adhirath was convinced that there was no use meeting him. Vermaji listened to their story with an air of complete concentration. Then he looked at Dalchand.

'Look, first of all these two matters are not connected,' Verma said.

'They are, sir, they are,' Adhirath jumped in. 'I did all this only for him, to save him. Do you get the point, sir? I was on leave. When all this happened I thought I must save him. How can they not be connected?'

Verma had gone very silent. Even after Adhirath finished speaking, he kept quiet for a full minute. Then he said calmly, 'If you have anything else to say, say it.'

'Sorry, sir, sorry. You know there is so much tension, he is so tense,' Nitesh said and pressing his foot on Adhirath's foot under the table indicated to him to keep quiet now.

Vermaji nodded. 'You are facing an internal enquiry. My client has a murder case against him. The defence we have taken is along a different line. Now if he goes as a witness for you and says he was with you on that day, he will be weakening his case. It won't help you either. I will say: don't involve Dalchand at all. If you want, I can refer you to some lawyer. There are many lawyers who deal with service matters. You can consult them. They can even appear on your behalf. See, Dalchand's matter is more serious. His life is on the line here. It is best to keep him out of this affair.'

'He will be questioned about this in the enquiry, for sure,' said Nitesh.

'Yes, he will. He will tell them where he was. How would he know what you did and where you were?' Verma said.

Adhirath thought Dalchand had begun to breathe again with relief. This constable, Dalchand, who had to obey his orders till yesterday, was today in a position to do him a favour and the bastard did not want to do it. Had his attitude been helpful, had he truly wanted to help, and had he said that the lawyer was tying up his hands, Adhirath could have understood. He himself would have told him to heed the advice of his lawyer. He would not have felt so humiliated then.

Adhirath was in such a bad mood when they got out that he refused to go back with Nitesh in his jeep. 'You go drop this Dalchand Yadav,' he said pronouncing the constable's full name for the first time. 'I have some work in Jafrabad.'

Dalchand said he would take the bus. All three went in three different directions.

Adhirath began hopping busses and for a long time he wasn't even aware which bus he had boarded and where he was headed. When he got back home it was past ten at night. There was a power cut. Slivers of light peeped from every house. To save the inverter power, all the members of every family were gathered together in the same room with only one light bulb and fan on. His heart sank. If he had to sit downstairs with the whole family, how would he be able to bear the tension? The efforts of the electricity department to unite families always peaked in the summer months. This would continue throughout the summer. He chose to walk down the road, braving the traffic and the noise. At last, when the light was switched off downstairs, he raced up the stairs and into the bedroom.

'If this is a trick to enforce family planning, it is a complete failure,' commented Pushpa switching on the fan. Now lights were off upstairs and downstairs. Only a fan whirred in both rooms. The inverter could be relied on for the next four hours. After that, they would have to sweat it out but they did not have to. Electricity was restored in three hours. Adhirath knew. For his eyes had not closed.

6

Why are there homes? Pushpa often asked herself. Now she was convinced that a home was designed as a highly sophisticated weapon to kill humans. If homes had been invented as a source of tranquility and rest, that concept had been buried a long time ago. Perhaps there had once been a prototype that had actually offered calm and peace but this must have been so long a time ago that even its fossil would not be available to thought-archaeologists. Ever since Adhirath had been suspended, the home had become a greater burden. She had no complaints against her in-laws. They were what they were, but Adhirath had changed so much. No laughter, no banter. They hardly ever went out. When he had been in charge of a police station, they could not go anywhere. Now he had all the time and she could get some leave of absence but even suggesting such a thing was like pulling the pin on a hand grenade. She felt she was walking on landmines. She used to think once the enquiry was over everything would return to normal. But ever since the notice arrived Adhirath had begun to disappear from home for entire days, returning only late at night. In the morning, he would drop Varun to school and vanish. When could she talk to him?

If she broached the subject at dinner, she was afraid he would stomp out, abandoning his food. And then he would turn such a stiff back on her that she could not say a word to him. That day she had decided that she would talk to him however late he came home, even if they had to be up all night. But by the time Adhir returned it was nearly ten. Daulatram, ever in search of an excuse to get drunk, grabbed this one. He had been drinking since eight. A large plate of salad, two bowls of namkeen and the fast-depleting contents of a bottle were evidence of his concern for his son. He began to scold Adhir the moment he returned.

'So you have begun practising the ways of a thanedaar? No time to dial your home and say where you are and what you are doing. Do you even remember that you have a wife, a child and a worried mother at home? The father is, of course, a useless fool...'

Adhirath escaped upstairs. Pushpa served the food cold in a thali and went up. By the time he came back from the washroom, wiping his face, she had poured rum in two glasses.

'You have made a lot of preparations today. Stole Bapu's stock, have you?' Adhir asked.

'Bought some. And you had to come so late today,' she complained.

Adhir downed the first peg as it were water.

'You have a lot of tension, no?' asked Pushpa and began to caress the back of his hand.

'You know we have nobody to back us up. Tell me how many Jatavs are there in the force? And whatever there are will not support me, they will only back off.'

'There is a way, I am telling you...'

'What?'

'I have thought a lot about this. If we get hold of someone...'

'I will go to jail. You'll take care of everything, won't you? How ashamed Varun will be.'

'Shut up. Nothing of the sort will happen.'

'It will take time. It will...' Adhirath poured himself a large one and began to take large swigs from the glass. 'You did very well, got this. SO good.'

'Where were you till now? Drinking on empty stomach can make you drunk very fast.'

'The world is a very bad place. A single woman is allowed no peace,' Adhirath said. 'They run her into a pross. You must be dealing with so many such cases on the helpline.'

Pushpa ate her dinner. She also managed to feed her husband a little. She could not do what she had planned to do. In the morning she took Varun to her father-in-law and placing his little palm in his hand said good bye to the child and called her office to say she had an upset stomach and would be late. When she took tea upstairs Adhirath sat in the room completely demoralized.

The moment he saw her he stood up and said, 'Will go.'

'Papaji has taken him to school. Sit down. I want to talk to you.'

Adhirath looked at his wife. A policewoman stood in front of him. Not in uniform. But that tone is unmistakeable. He did it himself, using that tone to make up for the missing uniform.

Pushpa said, 'I have taken half a day's leave. Unofficially. Let us discuss the enquiry.'

'You could teach a course in spoiling someone's mood early in the morning. Just when we're talking you throw that enquiry to my head.'

'If you run, your troubles will run by your side; you can't leave them behind.'

Folding his hands and bowing before her, Adhir said, 'Go on then. Have your say.'

'What is the point of talking like this? Do whatever you want to,' Pushpa exploded in anger. She turned and went downstairs. When he got down half an hour later she was ready to leave.

'Wait, I will drop you on the bike,' Adhir said. Without a word, she left the house.

Adhirath was still in the rumpled clothes he had worn to bed yesterday. Crumpled shirt. Crushed trousers. He got onto his bike the way he was and kick started it. Pushpa had hailed a rickshaw and was on her way to the bus stand. He followed her. When she got down at the bus stop he parked in front of her. She began to laugh despite herself and got onto the bike. He turned it to Madhu Vihar market where they went inside a sweet shop. Sitting at a table he said, 'Now tell me.'

'When we get hold of someone and bring him to the thana, what does he do?'

'Soils his pants,' said Adhirath.

Pushpa laughed again. 'He denies everything. Subsequently he is acquitted by the court also. You should also do this. Simply deny everything.'

'Really?' asked Adhir in a mocking tone.

'I have given it a lot of thought. If you deny everything the onus of proving it falls on them. Let them prove what they say.'

'You think you're very smart, no? But you're not an inspector yet,' Adhirath said coldly.

Pushpa abandoned her lassi and walked out. It was just as well that Adhirath had some money in the pocket of his trousers. He sat around for a long while sipping at his lassi. A waiter came several times to wipe the table but Adhirath paid no attention to his attempts to drive him away. He kept sipping at the lassi slowly. But it was only a single glass and at some point he had to finish and leave.

He had just reached home when his mobile began to ring. Nitesh was calling. He said he was coming that way so he would drop by. He had spoken to someone in the legal department and found out about a lawyer. Will come and tell him. And only today the wife had left without cooking. Pushpa had earlier planned to go late so she had postponed the cooking. Then she left without caring about lunch. His mother got up to put on daal to boil.

Daulatram seized the opportunity to ask: 'You could make barley rotis today. Should I get some barley flour from the mill?'

Adhirath called Nitesh on his mobile but he did not answer. He went upstairs and quickly changed into something presentable and walked up and down the road. The moment he spotted the jeep he ran towards it.

'I can't sit around here. Too much tension. Take me wherever you're going. We can talk on the way.'

Nitesh shook his head. 'Not possible, boss. This is official. Better I go alone. I'll be back in half an hour, max.'

Defeated, Adhirath went upstairs and lay down. He began to regret having been so harsh with Pushpa. Then he took off his clothes and went in to bathe and took a long time doing so. When he got out of the bathroom he simply could not sit in the room waiting for Nitesh. The tent house owners were once again loading the tempo. He heard the loud clanking of pipes as he came downstairs. As if they were mocking him.

'Saale, day and night you create a racket. Is this any place to live? Not a commercial place, this is. You have screwed people's lives,' he said kicking at one of the pipes. Then he bent and picked up a small rod of iron and flung it on the top of the heap of tent flaps. 'I will get your business shut down. What do you think of yourselves?' he screamed. Bapu came running. With great difficulty he dragged him inside the house. His mother was standing in the doorframe of the partition, her hands dusted with flour.

'You must keep on good terms with the neighbours,' she was saying. He shook off his father's grip on his arms and ran out, merging with the crowd and the chaos, striding away from his home. The mobile must have rung at least three times before he heard it. Nitesh was at his house. By now, some of his rage had gone down. He came back, trying to control himself. He saw Nitesh stab a puffed-up roti with a spoon. A bowl of ghee sat on the table. He poured the melted fat onto the roti with barely concealed greed.

'What daal, man! I just couldn't stop myself,' Nitesh said. He looked very happy though Adhirath could see that they were rotis made of wheat. Perhaps there had been no barley flour at the mill.

'You too come and eat,' said his mother. 'He is just so tense,' she said to Nitesh.

'I called that lawyer. We have to meet him at 3 p.m. Let us go.' He said biting into a fried green chilli.

Adhirath sat down to eat uninterestedly. But the first morsel changed his mood dramatically. He suddenly realized that he was terribly hungry. The roti was truly unequalled. He was eating a roti made by his mother after a long, long time. She patted the dough into shape with moist hands, without using a rolling pin or a board. Thick rotis, crisp on the outside and soft inside. One could eat such rotis with even a simple chutney and find them heavenly. Here she had served such a daal that you could drink bowls of it without any accompaniment. And that green chilli fried with salt. His irritation evaporated. He ate with gusto.

'The case is nearly cracked,' said Nitesh when they got into the jeep. 'I have got a warrant to search the farmhouse. That Parduman? He is the one who did it.'

'Really? And that Udairaj? What is his role?'

'He was at home only. We got the mobile traced. The whole day its location was the same. At night also the location did not change. It was in the house. He never left the house.'

'You apprehended him? Parduman?'

'Absconding,' Nitesh said. 'We are looking for him.'

Parduman could be on the farm. It would be easy for him to conceal himself; Cheti was so scared that he left at night to go sleep at Nachchatar's.

He did not tell Nitesh about his suspicions or his findings.

Both friends thought it strange that the grand building of the High Court would have such small rooms. Here sat lawyers who carried lakhs of rupees home every day, but why they had been packed like poultry in small enclosures was beyond their comprehension. They sat in the six square feet of the outer room on a settee with their legs drawn in to avoid bumping the other wall with their knees. Their legs began to cramp but they could not consider the possibility of going out for a stroll in the wide corridor outside. They did not know when the lawyer would ask them to come in.

'You can play cricket outside. That corridor is so wide. And here, if someone came in now he wouldn't find space to stand,' Nitesh remarked after twenty minutes.

'You heard him properly I hope. Did he say three o'clock?'

And then a man opened the glass door of the inner room and left the office.

'Come in,' said a pleasant man. This was Tarun Grover, advocate. He had never lost a case till now. Or so Nitesh had told him. Inside, Grover sat behind a massive desk. His black cloak hung from the back of his chair. Despite being thrice the size of the outer room, the chamber was still small.

Grover jumped up to shake hands with each of them when they introduced themselves.

'Sorry, you had to wait. I managed to squeeze some time for you with great difficulty. At three-thirty someone else is expected. But you see I can't say no to Tiwariji. He is in your legal department now but earlier he used to be my senior. I trained under him. Okay, tell me what is the matter? What brings you here?'

'Sir, it is like this. Over a year ago, I was posted as the additional Station House Officer of the Mandawali thana,' Adhirath began. He had rehearsed the summary of his case in his mind many times in the waiting room. Nitesh had warned him that Grover had very little time so Adhir would have to tell his story using as few words as possible.

Grover smiled and raised a smooth palm to stop him.

'I will read the story in the file,' the lawyer said. 'Simply tell me where the case is now. Only a departmental enquiry? That is what Tiwariji said.'

'Yes, that is what it is, at the moment. He said you take cases of service matters,' Nitesh said.

'Have you got the file?'

'File? There is no file,' Adhirath said.

'No file? There should be one. You must have got the notice. There will be an order for suspension. Always there is something in writing. Have you kept the clippings of what the newspapers reported in those days?'

'The enquiry is not concerned with what was published by the newspapers...' Adhirath began.

'True. Technically the reports will not be considered. But you see, everything together forms a picture. Anyway, you get the file. Tiwariji may have told you about the fees.'

'What is the need for the file? I am telling you what happened. In two minutes I will give the details. There is nothing in the file. It is this...there was a goon in our area. He ran a cable service. He had four charges of murder against him.'

The outer door opened. A man and a woman stood there, looking in. The lawyer raised his hand in a gesture that mixed apology with appeal. They retreated, closing the door. Grover turned to Adhirath and said 'Get me the file. Let me see what charges they have made against you. These matters are fought on technical grounds. Like when did they give you the notice? Was it within the stipulated period? Did they give you enough time to prepare for your defence? There is a procedure they have to follow when giving notices. We shall look into all of that.'

'Sir, they have asked me to appear next Wednesday. Today is Friday.'

'Bring the file tomorrow. See, we don't need more than half an hour to grasp the case. If I am not here you can give it to my munshi. And get the cheque for my fees. Thirty thousand rupees.'

Adhirath stared at the face of the lawyer for a few seconds. It glowed like gold.

'Sir, I have been suspended. How can I afford so much?'

'This is a question of your career. Don't think about saving money now. I will appear on your behalf. Tiwariji has recommended you, otherwise my fees are much higher. This is what I charge for one hearing. But for you I will deal with the entire case for just this much.'

'Sir, in one hearing they will arrive at a conclusion. This is not a trial in a court. Sir, if you find it tough you need not appear for me, give me only your advice. That will be helpful. For that, if you could please reduce the amount a little...'

'As you wish. All right. Get twenty-five thousand. And the file,' said Grover.

Nitesh and Adhir came into the wide corridor.

'Twenty-five thousand! That's a whole month's salary. Where am I going to get it from? You know my condition.'

'He is a big lawyer, Tiwariji was saying. You can't get an appointment in a hurry, have to wait two months. It is because of him that he met us so soon...'

'It's still a lot of money,' Adhirath said. He did not think he would have enough even if he emptied his bank account. It was just as well that he did not have to pay rent or they would be eating rotis without ghee. He looked at Nitesh. Nitesh got the hint.

'Listen, I am also...what to say...missus has no job. I have a daughter. Still, I can lend you some five or seven thousand.'

When they arrived at Udairaj's home, he was sitting in a back room drinking tea and watching TV. An English movie was on. His face went red with anger when he saw them.

'I wanted to ask you something,' said Adhirath. 'That girl, where did you meet her?'

'I don't remember,' said Udairaj, standing up. 'How many times do I have to answer your questions? Why don't you record them?'

'Sit down, sir. We have many questions to ask you,' said Nitesh.

'Why?'

'It is a murder case.'

'So? You are treating me like a suspect? Me?' Udairaj emphasized the 'me' with some annoyance. 'Are you in your senses?'

'It is our procedure, sir. We have to answer questions in court. The court will want to know why we didn't ask this or check that. Lawyers get paid only to harass us. Please cooperate. Where did you meet the girl?'

'You never told us, sir, how you met the girl,' Adhirath said smiling. Both of them were still standing.

'My driver brought her here some time ago. He said she was some distant relative of his. Parduman was the one who used to get her. I had to tell him to stop. I have told you all this before. You keep asking the same thing again and again.'

'What did she say her name was?'

'Something starting with an M. Yes, Mohini.'

'Sir, I have a warrant to search the farmhouse,' said Nitesh. 'You will have to come with us.'

Udairaj was taken aback.

When they left half an hour later, Nitesh asked Adhir at the corner of Lakshmi Nagar whether he should take a turn towards his house or did he want to go elsewhere.

'Keep going. I will tell you where I want to get off,' Adhirath said.

'Looks like we will be spending the night at the farm,' said Nitesh.

Adhir could see that he was not welcome as part of the search party. It was an official job. Nitesh had work to do. There were files piled on the back seat of his jeep. But Adhir wanted to go on sitting in the jeep, getting as far as possible from his house as possible. He felt that the farther he went from home, the fainter Pushpa's voice would get. He felt strangely restless.

Nitesh was on his way, his career running as smoothly as his jeep. On the other hand, Adhir had no work to do. He realized he was enjoying this investigation because he had no paperwork to do. All he had to do was talk to people and figure things out, without entering everything in a file. He did not have to brief public prosecutors and be lectured by them.

That had been true until yesterday. Today even the murder case was unable to hold his attention. No, no, he could see that he did not want this rest. He wanted what Nitesh had, what he had had till the suspension: a room next to the maalkhana, table, chair, cooler, hawaldars running errands and obeying orders. People used to ask him how much he had paid for such a plum posting, in the thana of his own residential area, where his house was within shouting distance. No one believed that he had not paid a penny. He thought that the department had thrown him there because it was notorious for its goons. He could not tell whether this was an insult or an opportunity. For such areas were the milch cows of the department. Only Adhir had not milked anything or anyone. This meant that he could not pay Grover thirty thousand. But then, he was not the type to milk such opportunities. If he had been the type who took money to settle cases, he would not have been in trouble that day.

Near Mehrauli he got off the jeep and onto the first bus he found headed towards him. It went inside Mehrauli village and he took a round of the bazaar. Shops were selling biryanis and kormas from huge deghs. He wanted to get some korma packed but the thought of his father discouraged him. Bapu would start cribbing: the spices were not fresh, the oil had been used several times, the meat stank.

When he got home Pushpa was rolling rotis. He sat down next to his mother on the bed and said, 'The lawyer is asking for twenty-five thousand.' His voice was loud. The intention was clear. Pushpa must hear this. The same stiff back faced him. It did not even tremble. Pushpa upturned the rolling board in the paraat, moved it aside, put the lid on the steel box with the fresh rotis in it, and placing it on the hot griddle under which she had turned off the gas, went out the door and up the stairs. He did not have the guts to go upstairs that night.

7

By the time Pushpa made the morning tea, he had got up. Having dressed Varun for school she said, 'Come back immediately after dropping him. We need to talk.'

Pushpa rarely spoke in the downstairs room unless there were guests. Her pots and pans spoke and they said a lot of things. The tawa getting off the stove, the pressure cooker letting off steam, spoons stirring inside pots, water being poured into jugs, every utensil spoke of the mood of bahuji. Today the kitchen implements were silent. Pushpa's words too were brief, precise. Adhirath left without a word. What would she do if he did not return immediately? Would apply for leave and wait for him? Unlikely, it did not look like she would waste her limited leave on him.

When he reached home, the tension had deepened. 'He is asking for twenty-five thousand. I have told her,' his mother said.

'I have some in the bank. I'll manage the rest from somewhere,' Pushpa said, ignoring her mother-in-law's words. 'But whatever you do, consult someone first. Don't do whatever you think is right.'

Adhirath suddenly exploded: 'Of course, I should do what you think is right. Listen to you. What do you care? You say deny everything. As if it is so easy.'

'Bahu is saying the right thing,' said Daulatram. He was in the sitting room but he could always participate in the discussion from there too.

'You did what you felt that is why you are in such deep trouble,' Pushpa hissed, gnashing her teeth. 'Who asked you to go buy this problem? You invited the bull to gore you and now that it has, you should at least get the right medicine.'

Adhirath came out in the sitting room.

'She says I should deny everything.'

'She is right. Otherwise, you are useless. You are the only Raja Harishchandra left in the world. Nobody says: Yes, I did something wrong. The worst of killers say they did not murder,' Daulatram said.

'Okay, okay, now you keep quiet, talk about this after a while,' Shakuntala was saying to Pushpa inside. The family was now divided among males and females but Adhirath felt as if everyone was ranged against him.

'Forget it. Let her have her say,' Adhirath shouted. 'Since yesterday she has been at it. Let her take out her anger. Let her abuse me as much as she wants to.'

Losing what little control she had over her emotions, Pushpa said, 'Do what you want to. It is not a question of the money. It is about your obstinacy. Let me tell you I am not going to put up with it. No way.'

'Why, what will you do?' Adhirath shook off the restraining hand his mother had laid on his arm. He moved menacingly towards Pushpa. It seemed as if today he would also do what only Daulatram had been doing in this house. He would hit his wife.

'First you listen what will happen to you,' Pushpa said, pointing a serving spoon at him. 'If you do what you want to, you will lose your job. You will go to prison. Prison. And don't think I will stay on to look after your family. I will leave with my son.'

'Hai Ram,' said Shakuntala hitting her forehead and flopping down on the cot. 'Have you heard? Arre, this is the custom in their caste. These people just take on another man whenever they choose. They go live with any man. I had told you to begin with...'

Propelled by the nervous energy his rage produced, Daulatram barged in and said, 'You will leave? You won't get a chance. We will throw you out right now. Here I am supporting her, saying Bahu is right, she is talking sense, and this bitch is showing the caste she comes from. Just grab her by the hair and throw her out...'

'Keep quiet, both of you,' Adhirath roared at the top of his voice. 'Selfish people, all of you, nobody is bothered about me. Yes, I will go to prison. You go where you want to go,' he threw his words at Pushpa and ran out to go upstairs. Pushpa left the stove burning and ran after him. For a while they could hear loud screaming from upstairs. Shakuntala had turned off the gas. After two hours Pushpa left for office and Daulatram went upstairs to check on Adhir and found him plonked on the bed his head held in his hands.

'When there is tension in the house, everybody tends to lose their heads,' he said. 'Come eat something and get some rest.'

'I will go to the lawyer. If you have some money please lend it to me,'Adhir said in a cold voice.

'Yes, of course,' Daulatram caressed his son's back. 'Whatever we have is for you only.'

In the late afternoon he called Nitesh and went to meet him. Nitesh lent him five grand like he had promised to do and heard the tale of his fight with Pushpa.

'Yaar, she may have said it in anger, otherwise she is very nice. Has a clear conscience. Don't take her words to heart. The advice she gave you is good advice.'

'So you too turn out to be on her side,' Adhirath said. 'Listen even in anger a person says what they have in mind.'

'Don't feel offended, but without you it is not easy for her to live there. All the time she is mocked at.'

'Has she said anything to you?' Adhirath looked at him with slanted eyes.

'Uncle keeps saying things about her to me,' Nitesh said. 'Says she is the only one who wants to implement Ambedkar's programme of inter-caste marriage. Do you know what he said once...let it go.'

'What? Since you have begun telling me might as well tell all,' said Adhirath.

'Yaar don't get too tense. All will be well. These things keep happening in the family.'

'No, tell me what were you going to say?'

Nitesh said nothing. Even after being asked many times he refused to tell Adhirath what it was his father had said to him. What could his father have said that he had not said in his presence earlier and many times? That she was of a lower caste, lowest of the low, with no education and no culture. They wear discards of others. They eat what others throw away from their plates. Here she wants us to use civilized language but in their caste they use foul language and abusive epithets even to call their children. Who knows perhaps she went with her mum and dad to collect garbage from people's homes. It is just as well that their mohalla is far away, had she been from somewhere close by they would never have been able to show their faces to anyone. In every house, garbage collectors come early in the morning.

Earlier they used to carry shit on their heads, yuck, nobody ever drank water from their hands. And if they ever asked for water to drink we used to give them water from the mug in the latrine to drink out of. Who knows, the bhangi from our mohalla may be their relative. Wouldn't that be great? He would come to collect garbage in the morning and it will turn out that our inspector son will be touching his feet, inviting him in and feeding him tea and biscuits. He had heard it all.

For a long time his mother had cooked her food separately. She would ask Pushpa to clean the bathroom. 'Scrub it with acid. You would be tirained to do it well.'

Nitesh was right. Pushpa had put up with a lot. In the beginning she used to tell him about how she was continually humiliated, she would cry sometimes. Then after she got to know the habits of her in-laws, she began to argue with them. Then she declared that she would cook and everyone would have to eat what she cooked. She was so stubborn about it that in the end everyone had given in. Only after a year, the untouchability had slowly disappeared from the house. But even now she had to hear a few taunts about her caste. So what was left that Bapu may have said to Nitesh that he cannot tell him? But Nitesh too was determined to not tell him so he quit persisting after a while.

'What happened to your case?' asked Adhir. 'Got to know for sure who killed her?'

Nitesh welcomed the change in subject. 'How can all the evidence be collected in such a short time? You have to handle other things too in a thana, you know. I am sure that driver did it.'

'Caught him or not? Is he still absconding?'

Nitesh laughed. 'Why do criminals do this? Why do they run away? If they had any sense they would not.'

'You may have evidence. He will be caught.'

'I got to know the very next day,' Nitesh said. 'I even talked to him. Brought him here. Do you remember that Mamaji from Hauz Khas? He had gone to drop him, that Parduman. I asked that Mamaji. Parduman dropped him there and left at about seven-thirty in the evening. Mamaji has a grandfather clock type thing. Apparently it tolled after he entered the house. Only once. So he looked at it and it was seven-thirty.'

It had not been easy finding this out when Parduman got back to Preet Vihar. There were so many cars parked there. Nobody in the house paid any attention to who came at what time. All the servants were inside. Even if they did step out, who had the time or even reason to check whether Parduman was back or not. Parduman himself maintained that he had gone back straight to Preet Vihar. He had reached there around eight-thirty and since there were many cars there, he had parked outside the colony, at the kerb.

'He did not go in to ask if anyone else wanted to go anywhere. Had he gone in would he not have to tell his employers that he was back? He would have to go in to at least return the keys to the car...' Adhirath said.

'I latched on to this very point. He said he deliberately did not go in. He was annoyed with them. They had ruined his Holi. Everybody was getting high on bhang and booze and he was sitting there in the car outside. Sometimes even the children ordered him about. Asked him to help lift crates of Coca-Cola or get milk or whatever. If he had gone in, he said, he did not know how many other people they would have dumped on him, asking him to drive them home. That is why he parked the car outside and went to sleep in it. He had thought he would take a short nap but when he woke up it was very late. So he slipped away quietly and went to a friend's house to spend the night there.'

'Meaning he shirked work, nothing else,' said Adhir. He thought there was something fishy about this explanation but he could not once again lay his finger on what was wrong. 'You did not give him a dose?' he asked Nitesh.

'Yaar, I haven't been able to find anything against him. Nobody on the farm says Parduman came that day. I asked in his neighbourhood and they all said he was home that morning. The morning of Holi. He lives alone. Unmarried. Had tried to molest some girls in the neighbourhood under the garb of playing Holi and there had been a scuffle with him too. There is a girl, who kept refusing to play with him but he grabbed her and rubbed some gulaal on her neck and also somewhere under it. He was beaten up. That is why people remember he was there. He left around noon. He has accounted for the night. It is possible after all that he wanted to avoid driving a lot that evening and had slept in the car. That friend of his, he also lives somewhere in that Jhilmil place, what is the name of that area, it is on the tip of my tongue and I can't recall...yaar, what is it called...yes, Bargadiya Gali. His friend lives in Bargadiya Gali and he said that Parduman had arrived in the wee hours. He looked exhausted. His clothes were all rumpled. He said he was unwell and went to sleep.'

'That is it. Yaar tell me, if you are unwell, will you go home or come to mine early in the morning?'

'I also thought it was suspicious. He said once or twice he had returned home late from work but he was given no time to rest. The phone kept ringing. He would switch off the phone but Sahib would send a servant to fetch him. That is why whenever he wants to vanish now, he simply goes to a friend's place. Sounds perfectly reasonable to me.'

'Even otherwise, nobody has seen anything. Who wants to appear as a witness...' Adhir said. 'The bloody janta wants the police to work but when it comes to being a witness they will all step back.'

'True. Yaar had it not been true that Satthiya kand would never have happened.'

Kand. Scandal. In which Adhirath was caught.

'Did he actually kill sixty people?' Nitesh asked him.

'I don't think so. He claimed that of course. Openly.'

8

Satthiya!

The whole area trembled in his presence. Nobody knew where he had come from. Some said he came from Amroha, some said he was from Bihar. It was difficult to say where he had arrived from. Not just in Mandawali, he was a feared man in neighbouring areas too.

He bragged openly: 'Nobody can touch me, I have killed sixty people—that is why I am Satthiya.'

Satthiya, from Satth, for sixty in Hindi.

He operated a cable network and whether you got the reception or not, you had to pay the full amount. He had many goons in his employ—small time criminals. A thin man. You could count his ribs, he was so thin. He always kept the top three buttons of his shirt open.

When Adhirath was posted in the police station, the first picture he saw in the file of habitual criminals was that of Satthiya. He wasn't much to look at. Medium height. Unremarkable features. But he was a history sheeter with a rap sheet a mile long. Drugs, rioting, wielding knives, there was not a major crime in the Indian Penal Code that he had not been accused of. It appeared as if he was out to prove that he had the skills for every kind of criminal activity. Had he not strutted around arrogantly and had people not given him the right to way, slithering out of his sight the moment they saw him, it would have been difficult to guess that this man in the dirty trousers ruled the area. The pavement sellers in the Monday Bazaar, the fish monger who set up shop on the slab of stone covering the gutter, nobody could run a shop without paying protection money to Satthiya. It was a working class colony. Small, single-room tenements were piled one on another in narrow lanes or around tiny courtyards and there were stories of many girls he had picked up and returned after a few hours or days. It was also said that even young boys too were not safe. Three murders had been committed while Adhirath had been posted there. The crime graph had climbed so high that it was difficult to justify their jobs and yet they could not lay their hands on any evidence. The only way to bring down the graph was to refuse to file first information reports but even that method had begun to fail. It was not possible that every crime was committed by Satthiya, but it hardly did any harm to other criminals to lay all of them at Satthiya's door and he himself never denied it.

After the first murder Adhirath had got him dragged to the police station and had had him thrashed the whole night. But the man was a tough nut. He never opened his mouth. Constables were scared of touching him. At least twenty or twenty-five people must have seen him commit the crime at the dhaba where Satthiya had gone to have his dinner. A little daal had splattered on the table, not on his filthy trousers. Satthiya issued an order, the boy who served him would lick it clean. The poor boy agreed to do it. He folded his hands and begged forgiveness several times. The dhaba owner came and pushed the boy to Satthiya's feet and admonished him. The more they tried to placate him the angrier he got. He cleared his throat and spat on the daal that had fallen on the table and said, 'Lick it, you mother...' The boy was frightened. He tried to turn and run away. Satthiya leapt at him, caught him from behind and ran his knife along his throat. A young boy who had run away from home and was scraping a measly living in the city. Nobody claimed his body. Who would risk his life for a nobody?

'Where are you from, you bastard?' Adhirath had asked Satthiya.

'Even my mother does not know whose seed I am, how can I tell you?' Satthiya had said shamelessly.

No use, his constables had told him. He has the backing of an MLA of a neighbouring state and that MLA has the backing of an influential minister. He supplies to them. Many things. It was said that the Minster was fond of boys of a tender age. Nobody talked of the Minister's taste in flesh but their eyes danced when he was mentioned. Who knows what else the man supplied. When things got too hot in the state for him, the MLA had helped him relocate and Satthiya had become a headache for this area in Delhi.

'Let him be what he is, this is Delhi, not a state that we will let go of a criminal because a politician asks us to,' Adhirath had said.

But they found not a single witness. The boy's body lay in the morgue unclaimed. After a month or so finally it was the police that cremated him.

By the time of the second murder, Adhirath had got to know Satthiya quite well. He had killed a shopkeeper. But it was a repeat of the same story: no witnesses. It was said that the shopkeeper refused to pay protection money, even after being threatened with death. Adhir would run into Satthiya on his rounds of the area. Sometimes he would be near the fishmonger who sliced fish in the light of a battery-operated lamp, sometimes eating aaloo tikki at the kiosk in the market, and at times perched on his motorcycle making catcalls and lewd gestures at young girls.

After the third murder, Adhirath had called him to the police station and had talked to him. This time it was a woman. Perhaps she had taken some small loan from him. She had a young daughter. One day Satthiya kidnapped the girl. The next morning he brought her back. And told them he would come whenever he felt like and take her away for as long as he pleased. When he went to her house three days later, he discovered that the woman had sent her daughter back to the village. Her son already had a job elsewhere.

The woman's body was found in her house. She was lying on her face, her sari raised above her waist, her throat resting on a small kitchen knife, her tongue sticking out, stained with her own blood. Even hardened policemen who had seen all sorts of murders found themselves trembling.

Adhirath took over the beating of Satthiya himself, kicking him viciously.

'Tell me if you have done it,' he had screamed. 'Or else we are bound to find out.'

'Like you found out the last time?' Satthiya had laughed long and loud. Adhirath had beaten him with his baton. 'One day you will die just like this, the way you kill others.'

'Why? Don't you like your skin or what? One day I shall peel it off of you,' Satthiya had retorted.

Adhirath had completely lost his head that day. How many abuses he had hurled at him. He was not even aware that so many of these he had tried not to hear his father use lay buried in his subconscious and were now pouring out like vomit from his mouth on Satthiya. Even his subordinates were stunned. They had never seen him so furious. They thought now he was coming of age, now he would become a true full-blooded cop.

Two inspectors had dragged him away. Afterwards Adhirath shivered for ten minutes. The shivering came back at night.

'One day I will kill him,' Adhirath had said.

The SHO had talked to him for about half an hour, explaining why this was not a good idea. Once Adhirath had calmed down, he understood. It was easy for them to say that Satthiya was a killer but the police had not even managed to find the murder weapon. Satthiya always kept it on him. After he slit the boy in the dhaba he had washed it with the water in the jug and pocketed it. The little knife they had found under the woman's throat had not been used to kill her, it was hers—her son had identified it—so Satthiya had used it, presumably, as a stage prop. The knife he had used to cut her throat and gash her tongue was still missing. Adhirath's job was to investigate. The job of punishing him was that of the court. How can any investigations be complete if the criminal places the weapon before the police and says, 'Yes, this is the knife I used, take it from me if you dare', and no witness would agree to say that they had seen the knife, seen the blood gush out like a fountain from the throat of a victim, heard a scream? The dhaba owner, said he was leaning inside the tandoor slapping rotis in it, how could he have seen anything? He heard a scream and looked up to see the boy lying on the floor in his death throes and soon he was dead. Who knows who killed him? The diners fled. They did not wait to pay their bills. The dhaba owner complained parenthetically that he had suffered a big loss. And was Satthiya going to take pity on him if he talked about his losses? Satthiya would charge the full amount. What use is the police, if he had to pay a criminal even after losing money?

Truly, Adhirath wondered sometimes, what use was the police? Nobody ever called the police station to say, 'Let Satthiya go,' but he never stayed behind bars for more than a few days at a time. The court kept upbraiding them saying their job was shoddy, they never completed any procedure, never filed a charge sheet on time...don't do this...don't you know how to do that? It seemed that Satthiya was on bail, permanent bail.

That is when Adhir discovered why he had got this posting so close to his house without paying a penny as a bribe. The police station required two SHOs, one for Satthiya and another for the other work of the thana. Everybody was making money hand over fist and growing fat.

Adhirath had been on leave. Pushpa had had a strange kind of fever. For two days she had been hospitalized. It was the second day after her discharge. He had applied for and got a full week's leave. He was at home. It was noontime. That very day he had got the cooler cleaned and had got new pads put in. He had put it on. The fragrance of water being sprinkled on the dry khus grass emanated from the cooler, making the room feel fresh and cool. Pushpa was dozing. Her gown rode over her thighs. His fingers played a little hesitantly on them, appealing for some responding quiver, some encouragement, some invitation. In the moist skin of an exhausted and weakened Pushpa recovering from the double assault of microbes and medicines, he had felt the half consciousness of awakening. The pressure of his fingers increased, Pushpa moaned, and sank into his embrace. Adhir was after all his name, he had to live up to the impatience the name denoted. He felt a frenzy overtake his hands. When did they get time to themselves nowadays?

Nights he spent with culprits in the lock up. Or doing it quickly and silently to not disturb the son's sleep. They could not afford to forget themselves and moan in ecstasy. And people are constantly talking of freedom of expression. Here you don't have the freedom to forget everything and express your love for your own wife. Their bodies were not in a mood to even tolerate the trembling air between them, they were merging into each other, forgetful of the world.

He really wishes he had not picked up the phone that day. But he had. The enchantment of the rhythmic movement of bodies and emotions was shattered. The salty taste of her perspiration behind his teeth faded away. He knows Pushpa has till now not forgiven him the treachery of that hot and fragrant day.

The money has been arranged. The full amount of twenty-five thousand. Bapu has given him ten thousand rupees. Who know why he had saved up so much money. Pushpa got fifteen grand. Her bank too must be empty. He had borrowed unnecessarily from Nitesh. But Pushpa is right, who knows, she said, there could be other expenses. Best to have some money in the pocket specially since there was a meeting with Grover in the afternoon.

Bharat called in the morning. He told Adhirath that he had heard that Parduman had come that night. He had been seen by four-five people. Adhir considered telling Nitesh but then he thought, 'It is his case, let him do the legwork. What is all this to me? I won't get a reward for apprehending the accused.' Then he recalled the honest open face of Bharat. He was an outsider. He could get into trouble.

He gave Varun ten rupees to go get himself a chocolate. 'Eat what you want to, beta,' he said. He saw a flash of happiness on Varun's face, but it did not look as if the child thought he had suddenly become a millionaire and could buy anything he wanted. He knows the value, or more accurately the devaluation of the ten-rupee note better than his dad.

He would have to hurry. At night the family talk had only been about the daily routine; the tension had eased but was not over. Involuntarily, his mind kept repeating the clichéd statement of the police spokesman on television, 'The situation is tense but under control'. He laughed to himself. Under control. Won't take much to get out of control.

The moment he saw him, Bharat said, 'You will jump with joy when you hear this. The pardhan and his ex-sarpanch friend, they had both seen Parduman. But forget them, the real witnesses are from another village.'

'Oh, ok. What news man! You turned out to be a real detective! Forget this property business and come join the force.'

Bharat looked gratified. 'You haven't heard it all. Come, let me show you something.'

Getting him to park his motorcycle at the station, Bharat got off and said, 'Come.'

Adhirath saw the bench on the platform. It was here that Ramwati had told him the story of her wayward daughter. How many people had Suryabala brought pleasure to but what did she get in return? Nothing but curses, even from the mother who had given birth to her. She had wanted to get out of the suffocating atmosphere of the village, find a place where she wouldn't be so judged. And yet, she had died in another village, so much like her own, at the hands of men who had used her, reviled her and killed her.

Bharat was striding ahead on the platform. Adhirath began

to follow him. Getting down from the platform, Bharat began to cross the rail line. Behind the rail line was a dusty piece of land. At one end of this field, where a broad footpath came down from the manned railway crossing, was a cluster of four tall trees. The footpath went round these trees towards the village. The village was a little distance away and on the other side of the station, so far that the station was not visible from the village. From the station you could only see a few old bushes of jhund and pieces of bricks and rocks strewn around in the field. Bharat stopped near the cluster of trees.

'This is what we call "Chaukhamba",' said Bharat, pointing to the four tall trees that stood like pillars in the four corners of the spot. 'Here, Parduman had parked his car. There was nobody here. The man who operated the boomer at the railway crossing must have gone to sleep. No villager was here. That is what he must have thought. But you remember what I said? Nothing remains hidden in a village. Three people saw him.'

Adhirath's thumped Bharat on the back enthusiastically.

'Great job, boss, great job,' he said.

'Let me tell you how I found this out.'

'Yesterday afternoon, Cheti came to meet me. After our evening party, I told him to come and spend time with me once in a while. The poor thing is lonely. The other workers are far away. He is the only one close to his farm. My shop is barely two furlongs from the gate of the Bindal farm. Cheti told me his problems. The mustard had been harvested and he did not know whether he was expected to sell it or get it pressed for oil. He had bought some seeds of gourds and had planted them to get some vegetables for himself. Nobody told him what to do with the farmland. Did they want to let it lie fallow or were they planning to plant something? Poor thing is very scared.

He says a ghost jumps from the mulberry tree at night. It must be her ghost. He can hear someone walking there. Sometimes he can hear pots and pans too as if someone is using them. Once he thought he had seen the lights come on in the empty and locked house but they went off pretty soon. He kept asking me if the girl had been properly cremated. If she wasn't, she must have become a ghost and must be haunting the place. He wants to quit his job. He asked me to find some work so he can go away,' Bharat said. 'We were talking about this when some Jhandapuriyas arrived. They began asking Cheti about Parduman. Cheti told them he had not been to the farm in a long while. Do you know, one among them said, "Where will he go if he lies to us?" So I asked him, "Why, are you about to buy a new car? Is that why you are missing the driver? Why are you threatening this poor chap; he is already shit scared as it is. He has begun to see ghosts here."'

'He is truly very frightened, the coward,' said Adhirath.

'You have to be afraid of the locals. Who is there to support these poor outsiders? I said if you want Parduman's number I can give it to you, why are you harassing this chap? The man is half dead because he has seen the ghost of the girl. All of them poked a lot of fun at Cheti.

'Since they were there, they sat down. They have nothing to do. Wear their shirts and pants and walk up and down the village road here in the market. Up and down. I said who knows that Parduman may have come on the day of Holi? Cheti wasn't around so there was nobody to open the gate for him. Must have had to park the car outside and all his arrogance must have taken a beating. That driver thought he owned the place. The manager also left because of him. They were smirking. And then the truth slipped out of one of them. He said that he had parked the car under the chaukhamba. One of them said: "That one who used to come here? He ran towards the farm like he was a thief. We knew from the way he walked that he was Parduman." The other two began to stare at him and then they suddenly tried to change the subject, to cover up for their friend's gaffe. They said, "It is not necessary that it was Parduman, the car to could have been some other car." I let it go, did not press for more. Why? You know it is not good to ask too many questions. Did I do good?'

Adhirath said that only trained and experienced CID people worked so professionally. Bharat preened a bit.

'When they began to leave I followed them. I said, "Why Zamidarji, I also suspect that Parduman had come but the question is was that fair maalik of his with him or was he alone?" The boys, they may have made a mistake but they are very clever. Said, "How do we know? We just saw a car under the chaukhamba." Great detective work, no?'

Adhirath felt a little disappointed. It felt like he had got hold of a clue and it had slipped through his fingers.

'So we know now that a car was here, it was parked at this chaukhamba. That is good. But Bharat bhai, this is no evidence that Parduman had come. The car could belong to anyone. Will have to investigate.'

Both began to retrace their steps. Adhirath noticed that Bharat looked crestfallen.

'Man, you have truly done something wonderful. Now all we have to find out is whether it was Parduman or someone else...' Adhirath said to buck him up. They crossed the rail line and came to the market. Adhirath had begun to be recognized in the bazaar and people called out to greet him with a Namaste and asked how he was. They sat down to have a cup of tea.

'Let us call Parduman. We will say we have seen his car. Had seen him too. And we shall ask for some money to keep quiet,' Adhirath said. 'You call him. Not from your phone. There should be a public call booth here.'

There were four payphones in Jhandapur Bazaar. But to use one of them was like announcing their plans on a loudspeaker. The shopkeeper would of course listen in and a few others would gather around to find out what was going on. So, both got onto the motorcycle and drove towards Chhatarpur. Adhirath dialed Parduman's number from a payphone in a shop there because Bharat said that Parduman would recognize his voice. Bharat began to chat with the shopkeeper to keep him from eavesdropping.

When Parduman picked up the phone Adhirath said, 'You are coming to the faram tomorrow? Get ten thousand.'

'Who is it?' asked Parduman. His voice sounded anxious.

'Tera baap. The car was near the chaukhamba and you leapt across the line. I saw. That girl also got out of the car soon afterwards. Should I tell the police?'

There was no response.

'Understood?' Adhirath asked.

'Tell me your name. Or whom will I pay?' Now Parduman sounded rattled. Was he trying to be clever or did he really want to know who to pay? Had the Jhandapuri youths already touched him for money? Was ten thousand too little? Should he have asked for more?

'Many saw you. Those three lads too. That is why I am asking for only ten now. Bring it tomorrow, I will tell you my name and address and everything else. Come by noon,' said Adhirath disconnecting the phone. To keep his conversation a secret he had cupped the receiver in his palm and thrust his lips inside the cupped palm, fairly growling into the piece. He had enjoyed it thoroughly even if it felt like an amateur stunt for a trained cop. He could have been a good actor, he thought, and here he was wasting his talent on a uniform. Bharat and Adhir came back to Jhandapur and had another round of tea.

'Time for a beer?' Bharat asked.

'I have to go somewhere today,' Adhirath said. 'Tomorrow. We shall drink tomorrow. Just keep your eyes peeled. For all you know someone may be hiding in the farmhouse. Is it Parduman?'

'The house is locked. If he is there he will need food, will have to come to the market. Cheti is so spooked, he's seeing things now.'

Adhir got Sunny Hair Stylist to give him a haircut. A crew cut. At the enquiry committee he would have to present himself with hair cropped close, like that of a policeman. Sunny gave him a good massage, sprinkling some water on his freshly cut hair, playing a drum on his forehead above the ears. He dozed. A feeling of wellbeing spread through him. He wanted a beer. But he had no time, he had to go and throw twenty-five thousand rupees away.

Grover took the bundle of notes from him and counted them carefully. He did not like taking cases of such low-level employees. They even got money stuffed carelessly in their pocket and pulled them out like a handkerchief. They would get twenty-five grand but would not spare twenty five paise for an envelope to put the bills in.

After Grover had counted the notes, Adhirath pushed a slim file across the table. It had the order for his suspension, the notice for enquiry, the photocopy of three sheets of the daily diary, and a photocopy of two pages of the attendance register. There were also clippings from four newspapers that had reported Satthiya's killing with headlines like 'Rogue cop slays unarmed man' and 'Vigilantism in broad daylight'. There was also a clipping of the editorial that had condemned the growing lumpenisation and anarchy of the police, which ended by expressing the hope that the government would punish these policemen severely. 'Such an unconstitutional act strikes at the roots of constitutional democracy. However dangerous a criminal the police cannot be granted the right to take his life,' it sneered.

Grover opened the file, glanced at the papers inside, at the daily diary and inspected the attendance register carefully. He opened his drawer and placed the currency inside and said, 'What happened that day? Tell me the whole truth. You may have heard that you should never hide anything from your lawyer and your doctor.'

This is the beauty of the black coat! That day Adhirath had come prepared with a short and succinct account, but Grover hadn't been interested in hearing the story, saying these cases are fought on technical grounds. Now he has seen all the papers and grasped the technical grounds but he wants to hear the full story because there is money in his drawer. Adhirath heaved a sigh, looked at the door and licked his dry lips.

'I have time,' said Grover, and getting out from behind the table he opened the door a crack and asked his munshi to get them some water and told him not to let anyone in till the client had left.

'Sir, the case is that there was a gangster called Satthiya,' Adhirath began. 'Lumpen, filthy lumpen. Would kidnap girls, kidnap young boys. Took protection money. Used to supply drugs also. Small time but he was a peddler all right. He threatened the pavement shopkeepers and took money from them. Used to run a cable service. Peddled smack also. He had the backing of a politician from a neighbouring state. That is what was said. You know the police knows all this but it can't prove anything. We knew what the man was up to but we never could hold him for more than a few days for we never got any evidence or any witnesses.' He knew he was repeating himself but he was now shaking with anxiety. The munshi brought in water and he downed the glass in a gulp and tried to calm himself.

Grover brought his fingertips together and locking and unlocking them said, 'So you guys got him killed. Hoon?'

'If we wanted to get it done, we would have done it a long time ago. When he killed that boy at the dhaba then these newspaperwalas did not come...'

'Which boy?'

'There was sir, a poor boy of nineteen or twenty. For a trifle this man slit his throat like you cut the throat of a chicken. Have you seen a chicken being slaughtered? You place a cut on its throat and throw it in a box and it flaps around for a long while before dying. That is how that poor boy must have died spurting blood. That dhaba owner, he was standing there and said he had seen nothing. He was so scared he did not even claim the body of his employee whom he may have paid less than minimum wages and exploited to the hilt. You know sir, when a dead body arrives, the IO has to spend a grand or two from his pocket. Get the body picked up, pay the driver of the cart. You know the bhangi charges a half bottle of rum for a postmortem. Doctors don't take cash but they will ask for something or the other.

Some will say get my mobile recharged so you spend 500 on that. Some will ask for the best quality shoes. Then you have to go looking for the parents of the dead boy. Does the government pay for all this? You have to keep pushing files with bills in it and after six months you may get a little bit of it back, that too after paying the accountant. We have to organize the funds ourselves. We paid to get his body released from the mortuary, and to cremate him, for the last rites. Five-six hundred were spent only on this good deed.'

'There is so much corruption,' said Grover withdrawing his hands with the interlocked fingers behind the desk.

'With an unclaimed body the cost can come up to two thousand five hundred or three thousand,' Adhirath kept saying.

'Where did your involvement begin? From that murder?'

'Yes. I caught hold of the goon. But nobody was willing to say anything. Had to let him go. He would threaten me every day whenever I ran into him. Had we wanted we could have bumped him off then. But our hands are tied. This job of the belt and badge is very bad sir. People think we have a lot of power but we are all hollow inside, completely hollow.' Adhirath was getting carried away.

'Come to the point,' said Grover, glancing at his watch.

'That is where I am coming,' Adhirath said. 'Who are we to get anyone killed? It seems he had a falling out with the MLA. Must have been blackmailing him. Actually, we don't know what was going on between them. But it so happened that my wife fell ill. I took a week's leave. She had come home from the hospital. I was at home only. The ASI called me to tell me the news that Dalchand had shot the bugger dead. He knew I hated the goon a lot. So he thought he was giving me good news. I ran to the thana sir. I took out the attendance register and signed my attendance in it. I also noted in the daily diary that Dalchand was with me on a round of an area far away from where Satthiya had been killed. The SHO was not in the police station. Then what? There was a lot of hulla bullo in the press. Reporters arrived at the thana. I told them that Dalchand was in Bargadiya Gali with me on the regular round so how could he have been in two places, how could he have killed anyone? On top of it, constables don't even have a gun on them. They are not given service revolvers.'

'Interesting. So whose revolver was used?'

'A country made gun was used. It had been sent to the thana.'

'From the maalkhana?'

'No. Had it been from our stash of case property, would we not have been caught? I just told you sir, the piece was specially sent to us for the job. It was new. Was sent by whoever wanted to get the job done. Politicians do this quite easily. A goon should also know his place. He can't beat the super-goon. Dalchand was in mufti, in plainclothes.'

Grover shook his head. He had heard many such stories and every time he thought how different even similar tales are.

'So you rushed to save Dalchand, provide him an alibi.'

'That was the mistake I made, sir. Did it in a fit of enthusiasm. It occurred to me later that if it was planned, Dalchand would have an alibi ready. The SHO had gone to court to appear in a case. He had shown Dalchand to be with him. After the murder Dalchand rushed to the court and wore his uniform there. That day he appeared in the court by the side of the SHO. The public prosecutor saw him. Ahalmad saw him. I was proved wrong. When there is pressure there is enquiry. Or else the matter would have been forgotten. We were the ones who had registered the FIR of Satthiya's murder. We never found the country made pistol. It had been returned. And it had been broken into components. The pipe was taken out and another fitted in its place. Evidence erased. It is difficult to organize all this at the level of a thana. There were people with more power, above us, involved in it.'

'Hmmm,' said Grover. He had understood the whole case but he had to give the client some value for money. When the goat himself was rushing towards the butcher to sacrifice his life, who would be foolish enough to spare him? The matter had been investigated. Everyone knew that the additional in-charge of the police station suspected that his constable had committed the crime, that he had tampered with the records to save his subordinate's skin. Such men are dangerous. They are capable of doing anything. And so a departmental enquiry had been ordered and the man was sitting across the table asking what he should do.

Grover studied the file. In the attendance register Adhirath had inserted his name between two names in very tiny letters and signed there. As the number four. Below it the number 4 had been altered to make it look like 5 and it was so clearly tampered with you could not fool anyone. The numbers after this too had been changed till it reached the serial number of 9. The serial number on the next page began with 9. That had not been changed. The second page was neat. Nothing had been changed on it. Only the serial number 9 being repeated was suspicious but it could be attributed to a mistake on the second page, beginning once again with the number 9.

'All these serial numbers here, have you done all this over writing, turning 5 to 6 and writing 7 above 6, all this? You did all this?'

Adhirath nodded. There was no over writing in the diary but it was written in very brief that they were going out to patrol the area. There was something strange in the column noting the times of activities. The officer writing above Adhirath's had put in the time as 12.35 p.m. Below this Adhirath had made an entry of a round and entered the time as 12.10 p.m. The time of return was shown as 2.37 p.m. But that was much later, after many other activities and their timings had been recorded.

'Many evidences there are against you,' said Grover. Adhirath's heart sank. What was new in what he said? He has to find a way out of the mess he had landed himself in.

'If you take my advice, you will say that you had continued to be on leave. Who knows who did what in your name? You do have the application for leave in the records don't you? In their file? In your superior's file? It was sanctioned, right?'

'I took out the application from the file.'

'Why!' Grover was taken aback.

'I tried to show that I had taken leave for only three days and joined when I was supposed to. On that day.'

'You could have done that without taking out the application from the file. You could have shown that you joined early.'

'Then they would have definitely suspected that I did it deliberately to save Dalchand. That it was part of a plan. I had to show that everything was natural, routine.'

Grover stared at him, incredulous.

'Okay, it does not matter. We shall return the application to its place. Your SHO should help you out.'

'He perhaps would. But I tore it up.'

The man seemed determined to lose his own case.

'Tell me,' said an exasperated Grover, 'Why would you do that?'

'Sir, it is our duty to look after our subordinates. I thought Dalchand had a fight with that bugger and shot him in the heat of the moment. It never occurred to me that all this could have been planned to its last detail. I made a mistake sir.'

'Now there is only one way out. Deny everything. Tell them this is not your handwriting. Let them get it examined. That will take some time. Even if the handwriting expert's report goes against you we shall go to court. Right now you say you were looking after your missus.'

'Dalchand will not be a witness for me...'

'He has to say what was planned for him. What can he do? But he will not depose against you. He will only say he does not know what happened or who wrote what in the register, for he was out.'

Exactly what Pushpa had advised him. When she advised him for free he paid no heed, her words carried no weight, he had even humiliated her. To get the same advice he had paid good money to a man who was not going to appear for him because he had reduced the amount of his fee. Or maybe because this was one case this man could lose. Adhirath left feeling cheated.

9

It was half past noon the next day when he ran into Bharat in the bazaar. At the booze shop.

'It won't be good for me to go there,' said Bharat pocketing the half bottle of rum. 'Beer is too expensive and has no kick in it either.'

'Has he come?'

'Looks like he has. The car is not here though. Cheti had come again in the evening yesterday. Says he will quit the job. He did not sleep there at night. Went to Nachchatar's. I just saw Parduman, inside the gate. About an hour ago.'

'He hasn't arrived today. He's been staying here only. Has he no driving to do?' Adhirath mumbled to himself. He dropped Bharat a little distance ahead of the station where his scooter was parked. He drove back to the farmhouse but killed the engine before he got to the gate. Dragging it he walked slowly to the gate that was half open. He kicked the gate open and dragged the bike in and parked it to one side.

Today even the bungalow was open. When he went in, he was impressed by the simple elegance of the place. There was no heavily carved furniture. Everything looked like it was made of unpainted or even unvarnished wood. The table was a roughly cut irregular slab of stone resting on two tree stumps;

no attempt had been made to smoothen them. Adhirath thought that the table was covered with dry leaves and wondered how they had come to be there. And then it dawned on him that the stone was an unusual one. It was not the marble of every middle-class dream. It was studded with the skeletons of leaves shed hundreds of years ago that had become part of the texture of the stone. The sitting room was a museum of such stones. Some of them were studded on the walls too.

'Fossils,' he heard a voice saying. Parduman stood at the door leading to an inner room. He had a sarcastic smile on his face. He was smirking at Adhirath's obvious ignorance. 'Perhaps you know what a fossil is?'

Fossils. The remains of life preserved in stone. He could see Saroj's taste stamped on every detail of the place. In the lamp shade made of the wire basket, in the handmade copper pots, in the brass lota, in the bronze figurines and above all in the unplastered walls which were not smooth but sandy to the touch, almost as if they were walls of a hut in a village.

'You are not from the village,' said Parduman.

All at once Adhirath found his police training asserting itself.

'I will ask the questions,' he snarled 'You're Parduman, right?'

Taken aback by this tone, Parduman nodded.

'Sit,' said Adhirath using the 'tu' for him. His tone made it clear that this was not the affectionate 'tu' used with familiar or junior acquaintances but the humiliating one used for servants and riff raff. He sat down on a chair shaped like a veena and pointed to a chair and gestured rudely to Parduman. 'What did you think? You won't be caught? You are the one who committed the murder. Now tell me why?'

Parduman remained silent for a while. Then looking over Adhirath carefully he stammered, 'Who are you, sahib? Are you in the police?'

'You will not ask the questions, bugger. Want a tight slap?' Adhirath added after a brief pause, 'The Jhandapur people called you, right? Did they or did they not?'

'Sahib I have not done anything. If anyone says anything...'

'Have you got the money?'

'What money?'

'Ten thousand. You had been told to get it.'

'I have it. You take it, sahib. Have they sent you? Inspector Nitesh? I could have brought the money there.'

Adhirath said in a menacing tone, 'Bastard, I told you, I will ask the questions. Just reply to them. That night you got the car here and parked it under the chaukhamba?'

Parduman was still standing, towering over Adhirath. His chest was broad. His arms looked like he worked hard at weights. He was not wearing his chauffeur's uniform. He wore a blue T-shirt and black trousers. He could have easily tackled Adhirath but his guilt and his suspicion that the man was a cop robbed him of all his strength.

'The Inspector will let you go for ten thousand! Is that what you think? That too in a murder charge? Come, now let me hear your story.'

Parduman sat down and told him the story.

For ten years he had served Udairaj and Saroj Madam as a driver. In the beginning, he regularly brought Saroj Madam to the farm. She came here at least three times a week. Not just here, he had driven her to Agra, Shivpuri and wherever else she wanted to go to pick up things to build this house. She had selected each and every stone personally. Taking her to these places, he had also developed a taste for the good things of life. He had eaten such fantastic vegetables from the garden of this bungalow that he could not even dream of seeing in this life. Once in the bazaar he ran into Basanti. He had gone to fetch milk and offered her a lift.

'She didn't live in Chandola,' said Adhirath.

'No, I dropped her off at Amirpur,' Parduman said. He said that the police had told him recently that Basanti's real name was Suryabala. He did not know this. She had told him it was Basanti. Had he been friends with the villagers, he would have discovered her name and many other things about this butterfly. But he kept his distance from the villagers. She wore parandas. Then she stopped wearing them and let her hair down. Soon she began to experiment with buns and chignons. Sometimes her hair would be ruler-straight; sometimes wavy and once, she had tried tiny curls, so that her hair became a halo. That was how he had seen her the first time, with her hair clustered in tight curls like a cloud. He mistook her for a woman from the city. She was buying samosas and he said 'Namaste'; she nodded stiffly. He did not see any car around and thought she had walked up from one of the farmhouses close by and offered her a lift. It was only when she got into the car that he realized his mistake. For she came and sat in the front seat. No owner of a car would do that with a driver. He was in his chauffeur's uniform and a farmhouse Madam would sit in the back. Then she opened her mouth to speak and the truth came spilling out. She was from Amirpur, she was low-caste, her English told him that clearly. But she was very pretty. And so Parduman noted her phone number. He learnt that she seldom came to the village, that she lived in Chhatarpur on her own in a room and worked for a parlour. The woman who owned the beauty parlour had a store room that she had rented to this girl to make a little money. Who else would have rented a single woman a room in the village?

A week later he brought her to the farmhouse to show off. After that whenever he came to the farmhouse, he would see if she were free and bring her with him. While the caretaker plucked the vegetables, they would have fun in the bedroom. Parduman made a lot of money on the side. So he began to shower gifts on her. She would come with him in the big car and would go back with him. But she wanted a lot more. More money. More clothes. Jewellery. There was no end to what she craved. She wanted to have expensive things, she wanted even her underwear to be expensive.

'Sahib, tell me now, are you in the police?'

Adhirath deflected the question with a stern look and said tersely, 'Continue.'

After that Parduman and Suryabala kept meeting. Parduman had a set of keys to the farmhouse so that he might keep the house clean and maintain the wall. 'These walls have both cement and dung. It has to be given a coat of the same stuff once in six months or so. It is skilled work. Not everybody can do it. In Taimur Nagar in Delhi you can find some people who know how to do this. They are from Rajasthan and they are the ones who made this wall. Saroj Madam had found them. I used to go fetch them here and even drop them back once they had finished the task. I had a lot of freedom and time to do all this.'

'They also had a manager here,' said Adhirath.

'Only in name, sahib. Only in name. Now tell me who got seeds from Indira Market? Parduman. The tubewell has to be serviced, who will get it done? Parduman. For a whole year I alone came to this place. I carried back the vegetables and fruits.

The manager only organized the extra labour and paid them. Yes, he knew when to get the tractor to plough the field and he took it to fill it with diesel. He knew when the planting had to be done. He made sure that the workers worked properly and were paid on time. All that he did. But the running around, the real hard work, I did it.'

'So you began to enjoy yourself.'

'What enjoy, sahib? Sometimes I would bring her and have a little fun. That is all. Udairaj sahib had no interest in the farm. He would go to the factory, to the mall, to the club but he would never come here. He came only once for the grihapravesh. Madam is the one who is fond of this place. She was truly fond of it.' He kept quiet for a while.

Adhirath cocked an eyebrow at him.

'I am telling you, sahib. One day I don't know what happened but Udairaj-ji came here all of a sudden. Those days that Nachchatar used to work here. He was a real bastard. Never even came in to warn me. After all, he must have opened the door for him. And sahib barged into the bedroom. You know, we were lying in bed, after doing it, no clothes on, all that. I thought I have lost my job now. But sahib, I got saved because of Basanti. The next day sahib calls me and what does he say, "Call her to the farm". After that Udairaj sahib began to make trips to the farm quite often. His factory was anyway about to shut down. Later it did. Sahib got the locks to the house changed. After that this became his den.

'One day I took her to sahib's house. She insisted that I show it to her. I told Saroj Madam that she is some distant cousin and has done a beautician's course, you give her an opportunity to work for you and maybe later you can get your friends also to call her home. Sahib got very angry. He came here and hit her, slapped her hard. "Stay within your limits," he told her, "if you ever show up at my house I will teach you a lesson you will not forget." Then he told me if I brought her there again he would throw me out.'

Parduman told Adhirath that he used to lie down on Cheti's cot in the back and Udairaj would enjoy Suryabala in his bedroom. He had no objections to Udairaj sleeping with her, after all she was not his wife or lover. He had a good job. The money was good. He got the fanciest of cars to drive, he was truly fond of driving and the cars mattered to him. Girls he could find plenty but such an easy job would be hard to land. Udairaj did not come every day so he too had his turn with the girl. 'Sahib knew about this but he never said anything. Who cares who sleeps with a whore?' he asked rhetorically.

But it was too good to last. After some time, Suryabala lost her head completely. She began to treat Parduman as if he were her servant. When he went to fetch her, she would sit in the back of the car. She ordered him about. She wore goggles inside the house and never took them off. But Udairaj had not given her his mobile number. He never called her himself. He always used Parduman's phone to call her over. Once Parduman called her and said sahib wants you to come, and took the car to bring her over. But Sahib was not here. That day she fought a lot with him and said she would complain to Udairaj. That he would never be able to trick her again for she would never get inside the car if Udairaj was not in it.

'I even beat her up and made her sleep with me. I sent Cheti away on some errand and fucked her in his room. She was screaming that she was now too good to do this, to lie down on a filthy sheet. I wanted to tear her apart. I could see what she was thinking. She thought Udairaj sahib would marry her.'

'And would he have?'

Parduman looked incredulous. 'That is why I took her to his Preet Vihar house two or three times. So that she could see for herself what her status was. Nobody even talked to her. On her way back she said, "What an ugly woman has been hung around your sahib's neck. He will definitely leave her, soon and he will marry me." I told this to sahib and even though he was angry with me, he was angrier with her. He called her from my phone and warned her. He said, "If I see you anywhere near my house again, I will serve you to my friends." Serve you. That is what he said, the exact words. He also said prostitutes don't enter our houses. Yes, that is what he said. I heard it all.'

After that she got close to Parduman once again and began to complain to him about how she was being treated, like a piece of flesh. She began to want to avenge herself. She also began to make Parduman happy the way she used to earlier. He used to go to her house now for he no longer had the keys to the farmhouse. 'But one night she stole the keys from Udairaj sahib and passed them on to me. I got a copy made from this very bazaar while they were locked inside the bedroom till noon.' After that he too had access to the bedroom once again.

When she became pregnant Parduman told her that they had a good opportunity to make a lot of money. He told her that once she got money he would marry her, they would go away somewhere and he would find a new job. They wanted to make at least twenty-twenty-five lakhs. Basanti had begun to dream of even more. If the child turned out to be that of Udairaj, she would demand a share in his property. She had heard women discuss something like this in the parlour. They said that whether the man had married the woman or not, if the child was his he would have to give the child a full share in his property.

'Is it true?' he asked.

'Go on with your story,' said Adhirath in his cop voice.

There was no guarantee that the child was Udairaj's. It could just as well have been Parduman's. But that did not matter. The threat itself would have worked. Udairaj would do anything to save his reputation. Parduman had no intention of marrying this kind of woman who, for all he knew, was carrying someone else's child. His plan was to get rid of Basanti. She could meet with an accident. That is when Udairaj himself asked him to get rid of her for him. 'She had stolen his diamond button. He told me, "Thikaane laga do." After sahib asked me to do this, I changed my plan.'

He told Udairaj that a professional killer he knew would charge five lakhs for the job. Udairaj gave him two lakhs. Told him he would pay another two lakhs after the job was done. Parduman planned to kill her in the farmhouse and plant enough of Udairaj's things on her as evidence so that Parduman could avenge himself too. But at the last moment everything went horribly wrong.

'That night, the night of Holi, Udairaj sahib had called the girl here. He came here. That was who people saw.'

Adhirath got up and walked over to where Parduman was sitting. He placed both hands on the arms of the chair and bending over him threateningly, said, 'Do you take me for a fool? Look at your height. Udairaj is at least a foot taller than you. He is slim and you are hefty. And people got mistaken?'

That is when Adhirath's phone began to ring. He fished it out still bending towards the driver, who could see clearly Nitesh's name on the screen. Adhirath took the call. Nitesh wanted to know if he had met Grover and what was the outcome.

Adhirath said deliberately, 'Yes, man. I am at it.'

Nitesh asked him if the lawyer had found any evidence in his defence.

'Evidence is what we are gathering,' said Adhir again, deliberately trying to mislead Parduman whose ears were cocked. 'The rest of the case is clear, isn't it? Listen man, will talk to you a while later.' He disconnected the call.

Pocketing the phone, he looked at Parduman. 'Come let us go to the police station. We'll talk there.'

Fear widened Parduman's eyes. 'Sahib, I am telling you the truth...'

'And what the pradhan saw? Is he also lying? You may have an identical twin who was here that night. That ex-sarpanch. He has a habit of lying, doesn't he?'

Parduman slid off the chair. Adhirath had seen such a miracle many times, the spine of a hefty man slipping out of his body, but every time it gave him a thrill. The validation of his power and authority made him forget the many disadvantages of his job.

'I had come here sahib, I had. But I left the girl here in the house and went to sleep in Cheti's room.'

'Why did you not drive up in the car?'

'Sahib...Udairaj sahib had asked me not to.'

'Tell me the truth now. You went to Hauz Khas. After that?'

Parduman told him that he had called Basanti during the day. He had asked her to come to the farmhouse. She began to put on airs, saying it was Holi and getting there would be difficult. She refused to take the train, insisted that he pick her up. Most of the times Udairaj used to go with him so they used to pick her up from somewhere near the parlour. That day the parlour was closed.

'I had taken sahib's car to drop Mamaji. Then I picked her up from the bazaar near her house. Just before the railway crossing, I made an excuse that the car is not moving, there may be something wrong with it. I let it slide down the incline on the footpath and let it come to a stop near that cluster of trees. Then I asked her to wait in it. Told her I would go ahead to check if the bazaar is open. If it is I will get back, if it is not, I will stop at the station and wait for her to join me. I told her it is the day of Holi, the villagers may be drunk and they may molest you. She agreed. They used to harass her a lot. I went ahead and stood at the station. After about fifteen minutes she got out and followed me. I kept walking ahead and she followed. We walked wordlessly. It is a little over a kilometre, did not take us long to get here. We had been here a very short while when those two came in. They had seen the light in the window. There was no car. Or else they would never have dared come in.'

'Then?'

Parduman went silent on him. Then he got up and said, 'I'll get some water.'

Taking hold of his arm and twisting it, Adhirath pushed him to the wall. 'You will go when I tell you to. What happened after that?'

'What could I do, sahib? It was not my fault. They both, in front of me...I got out of the room. She did scream a little. Then she stopped. Maybe they stuffed something in her mouth. They worked her over for half an hour or so. Could be more too. Then they left.'

'And you are a saint! We have evidence of three men having done her.'

'I admit it, sahib. That was the first thing we did when we got here. She had begun to show a lot of arrogance ever since she got between Udairaj's legs. One day, she told the manager, "I am going to become your mistress." There is something you should know, sahib, that woman was so good in bed that once a man had her, he got addicted to her. He would never want to leave her. That is why I used to feel bad. When she slept with me, I could tell the difference. She did it only to keep me on her side. You can tell when a woman is doing it with her whole heart and when she is doing it half-heartedly. She would not give me full satisfaction. That day the moment we got here, she said to me, "I don't like living in that dirty room above the parlour. Let me have the child, then I will move in here. Otherwise, I will make him buy me a plot of land nearby, you just wait and see. And you can take me out for a spin." I went crazy with anger. Pushed her on to the bed. Showed her how much strength I have in me. When I got up that pradhan and that sarpanch were standing at the door. We had forgotten to bolt the door from inside. Those two had a free ride.'

Adhirath's slapped Parduman, a resounding slap. Parduman was hefty and could have broken his hand in no time but Adhirath was dominating him now because of his own misunderstanding that Adhir was a cop in mufti, questioning him officially, and would bung him in the lock up soon. Actually it was not even a complete misunderstanding.

'And you say Udairaj came here? When?'

'They had just got out of the gate when he arrived. I was going in and the bitch came out. She was screaming loudly. That is when Udairaj came. He caught hold of her plait and pulled her. I ran away.'

'Which car did you go back in? In the one you had parked near the chaukhamba or the one that Udairaj had come in?'

'He did not come in a car. I had gone to shut the gate and he was standing there. He said that he had guessed that I had got a copy of the keys made and had come to confirm his suspicion. I left on foot. Went up to the car and sat there under the tree for a long time. I don't know what happened here. Truly, I swear.'

Sitting on the floor, Parduman hid his face in his hands and burst out crying.

'Now you listen to me carefully,' Adhirath said to him bringing his face close to his. 'You know why we have not taken you to the police station to interrogate you? We have to get money from you. Understand?' Parduman nodded. 'We know everything. We know that you were the one who cut her up. If you tell me the truth I can even tell you a way out. We also know that you have been staying here for so long. That day Cheti had also seen you and I had seen you too. I kept quiet. You were here, were you not? Behind those trees? Now tell me how much money you got from Udairaj and why you cut her up? You say Udairaj had throttled her. But he did not wield the knife. That much I am sure of. Now tell the whole truth. That is the only way out for you.'

'Sahib, I told you all...you are a policeman...' Parduman began to beg for mercy.

'Will you tell me all or shall we go to the thana?'

'Sahib when the pradhan and sarpanch came I had postponed the plan to kill her. I had two witnesses to place me here. When the two finished with her and were leaving I thought I would take her back. But everything went wrong. First she came out screaming "I am not a randi". At that moment Udairaj arrived. He may have seen the two leave the place. Two villagers had screwed his mistress in his wonderful bungalow on his bed. The very thought made him furious. He said, you bastard, you copied the keys and now you have turned my house into a brothel. On one side Basanti was screaming that she would tell everyone, she would go to the police, she would make sure we would not be able to live in peace and I don't know what else. To shut her up Udairaj pulled her dupatta around her throat. There was some struggle. But he pulled very hard. Here, near this window. She clawed at him but he tied it round her neck like a noose and pulled very hard. She ran towards the trees trying to wriggle out of it and collapsed there. She may not have died, maybe she had only fainted.'

That must have been when a corner of her dupatta got torn in the struggle. The button too must have got entangled in the threads she had tied around her wrist and come off. She must have struggled very, very hard. But the button had been stolen earlier. The driver had said so, Saroj had said so. Had she stolen another button? Then where did that one go? It was clear that Udairaj had strangled her and then Parduman had cut her up.

'You slit her open?'

Parduman remained silent.

'Where did the knife come from?'

'That knife. It was lying around outside near the other implements like the khurpi. You see that bay window? The one with the seat? Outside there is some space where khurpis and spades are kept. That knife too. It is used to gut and clean game,' Parduman said. 'Sahib was so angry he was saying, "Cut out the cur, that filthy puppy she is carrying and throw it away." He was standing here watching everything.'

Adhirath fell silent. He could not bring himself to ask anything. If his wife carried a foetus it was his son, and the one this woman carried was a puppy for him. A cur. Even if the seed comes from the same source, only respect for the womb can get respect for the child, he thought. How contempt for the womb can turn to contempt for one's own seed. A man's lust and lecherousness are legitimate but in a woman the same appetite turns into sin. Even his child was illegitimate because he had contempt for her existence.

Parduman began speaking again. He told him that Udairaj had taken the sheet off the bed, spread a fresh sheet on it and thrown the used one at his face and left. Parduman too had some clothes he kept on the farm. He changed his clothes. Picked up the knife and tied the clothes he had taken off in the sheet along with the knife and carried the bundle with him. He had also searched Basanti's purse but he did not find the diamond button in it.

'Diamond button?' asked Adhirath almost on auto drive.

'It belonged to sahib. She used to keep it in her purse. But I swear sahib, I did not find it.'

He emptied the purse of money and tied that too in the bundle. By that time the rush of adrenalin may have been over for he said he began to get the shivers and was very frightened. He simply could not remember to throw something belonging to Udairaj near the body and he left the place. It was after midnight. Then he sat around under the trees near the car and left once he had controlled his fear. It must have been over two hours later that he started the car, at least that is what it felt like. It was dark. Everything was still. Even the dogs had gone to sleep.

'There is that nullah after crossing Jhandapur, where you turn towards Chhatarpur, it has a bridge too, that is where I threw the bundle.'

'And the shoes?'

'Shoes?'

'Saale did you come here barefoot? Were there no blood stains on them?'

'I had taken them off. When I got into bed...when the pradhan came, I ran out barefoot. You get it? I did not have the time to even pull up my pants, I ran out somehow...got out and then put them on properly.'

Adhirath felt cold sweat forming on his forehead. Did the villagers have so much power? That they could enter the house of a rich man and do whatever they want with impunity? Even rape his mistress? Where could the poor woman have gone to escape such men? All she had to fall back on was her cleverness, and all she could earn was from the sweat of her labour, the services her body provided. And this man? He wanted to make millions, having stamped on her body. For Udairaj, she was only a piece of flesh he came to gnaw at when the need rose in him. He even said he would serve her to his friends. Serve, like a dish! To save some lakhs. He could not give the woman a few lakhs but he would pay a lawyer any amount to save his own skin. He could not buy her a small flat to provide for her but he would spend on expensive cars. Their greed was not greed. Their misconduct was concealed behind the curtain of wealth, behind the thick walls of their bungalows, behind the customs and traditions they had so carefully nurtured. She had no curtains; she had to live in the open. And this man, this Parduman. He did not stand by her side to fight the pradhan and the sarpanch. He abandoned her to them. Such a well-built man, one slap would have been enough to drive them out but he was showing her how much strength he had, that is what he said, using his brute strength on her, not for her. Had he fought back, what would they have done? Brought more people to assault them? Is that what he had thought? Is that why he left her to their mercy? Perhaps he had shown sense in acting the way he did. The car was far away. They could not have escaped in a hurry. Yet, Adhirath found not an iota of sympathy for his predicament.

If anyone protested it was only that lone woman. She scratched, dug her teeth in them, got beaten up, screamed, but who was there to listen to her?

'The blood must have sprayed your feet then?'

'I dipped them in the pond here,' said Parduman.

Were there still some drops of her blood in that pond lurking under the broad leaves of the blue lilies? Waiting to be put in a test tube? To nail her murderer? What would another drop of her blood prove?

'When is the water of that pond changed?'

'Every day,' said Parduman. 'It is emptied out to irrigate. If the grape vine has been given its water this year they will be really very luscious. When we hunted hares here we always gave the blood to the grape vines. Blood is very good as manure for them.'

Adhirath drove his fist into Parduman's stomach viciously. Parduman doubled up but did not scream. Adhirath felt like laying him flat on the ground on his face and stamping on his spine to break it. But Parduman was only telling him the truth, they had been drinking her blood to enrich their lives.

She was a luscious grape for them, who intoxicated them like wine. You got addicted, that is what he had said, both of them. He felt a strange feeling of revulsion in him. Suddenly he realized just how alone that woman was. He felt a strong desire to tie Parduman to his bike and race it, dragging him through the mud. The rising violence in him surprised him. He began to pace up and down the room. When the restlessness went down a bit, he sat down. Parduman was staring at him, alert and cautious like the mouse who knows the cat was not done playing with it, it will return to grab it.

'Tell me what you were eating here for so many days? You were here, were you not?'

Parduman admitted that he had been hiding here. It was easy. The first time he came here that night, before they went hunting. Cheti was away. He had just entered when Cheti returned and saw him. Scared he ran away and Adhirath came in after a while and when Cheti left with him, he had the place all to himself and it became easier for him to plan his stay.

He went round, opened the back door, then he came to the front and locked it from outside, returning inside from the back door and bolting it. He had got some bread and snacks with him. At night when Cheti would run away he would go out and get himself some vegetables. When Cheti spent nights away from the place he would light candles and cook himself something. There was some rice and daal in the kitchen. Once he had had enough time to kill himself a rabbit and cook it.

'The day the inspector came here to search the farmhouse, where were you?' asked Adhirath.

Parduman kept quiet for some time. Adhirath thought he was about to laugh at the stupidity of the police, and perhaps he would have, had he not been scared of Adhirath. His lips twisted a bit.

'I was here,' he said. 'When the jeep came, I heard it and ran out of the back door and hid behind the trees at the end of the farm.'

Even then, they may have noticed that the back door was not bolted. Did they not suspect anything? Could Nitesh have not noticed it? Had Udairaj seen it first and quietly slid the bolt in?

'How much did Udairaj pay you? This time the truth,' Adhirath said.

'Four, four lakhs,' Parduman stammered.

'How much did you pay the Jhandapuri youth?'

'Only fifty thousand till now,' Parduman said. 'They are asking for a lot sahib, full two lakhs.'

'Now my last question. What was Udairaj wearing when he came here that night?' Adhirath asked.

'Kurta. I don't know what colour it was. It may have been white. It was splotched with the colours of Holi. Kurta-pajama. He changed his clothes here. He wore another kurta.'

Adhirath picked up the ten thousand that Parduman now placed before him and handing it to him said, 'Keep it.'

'You want more, sahib? All the money is here, I have buried it here.'

'Take my advice. Go tell the police everything. You may get some leniency when the judge decides on punishment. The court may show some mercy.'

Parduman kept quiet.

Adhirath left him there and told Bharat the whole story.

'Parduman too must have lost his head. One, the villagers showed him how little he mattered, they did not even allow him time to zip up his trousers and went and jumped on the woman he had with him. On top of that, Udairaj accused him of turning the house into a brothel. He was going to lose his cushy job. He blamed the woman for this and cut her up. His clothes must have got drenched in blood. Udairaj was standing at a distance, he may have caught a few drops of the spray. He simply took off the kurta and gave it to the servant to get rid of it. A truly spoilt rich man.'

Adhirath did not feel like drinking rum. But a small drink with Bharat was necessary. So he poured himself a finger and gulped it.

'Yaar, tell me something...when people don't have their own vehicles how do they come here?'

'By train,' said Bharat.

'You can't get a train all the time.'

'No, you can't. In the morning there is the milk train. From six in the morning to nine many trains pass through. Local trains also. For milkmen. In the evening too you can catch a train. Trains keep arriving till quite late. If you walk a kilometre or two from Jhandapur Bazaar, you can also get a tempo. You get buses too. Tempos start plying early around six in the morning.'

Quite possible that Udairaj came by train or tempo with a cloth wrapped around his face. Pretending to be a Holi reveller. Somehow Adhirath could not imagine Udairaj putting in so much hard work to get here.

10

'I would say something if anyone paid heed. In so many years he never took my opinion seriously, not even once. Now that it is the question of our son's life, at least now he should have remembered what I had said. When the man called he should have at least asked,' Shakuntala Rani said as she chopped cauliflower, sitting on the cot across the kitchen counter.

Daulatram could not control himself any more. He came in and screamed, 'You have a lot of sense, don't you? I did say, but that man is not bothered about your son, he is only bothered about his niece.'

'Papaji,' said Pushpa keeping the washing she had on one side of the cot, 'I had asked Mamaji to do something. He did talk to the man but he said that a lot depends on what Adhirath says in his statement to the enquiry committee. Please knock some sense into him. Ask him to say what the lawyer has advised him to say.'

In the beginning when Pushpa had used her husband's name in the presence of her in-laws, her mother-in-law had reminded her of the tradition of seven generations never uttering the name of one's husband. She said that Pushpa should always refer to her husband with a pronoun and admonished her to mend her ways. Pushpa ignored her and continued using

Adhir's name. His mother then raised the issue with Adhir who shrugged. He didn't mind his wife using his name; he liked it, in fact. When his mother insisted, he turned on her.

'Either we live here as we want to or we can get government quarters. What will we lose? House Rent Allowance, na? But at least we will be able to live the way we want to.'

Pushpa glowed gently at this.

She knew it was an empty threat but neither Adhir's mother nor father called his bluff. Now they were used to this new-fangled way of addressing the husband by his name, of the wife using the intimate 'tu' in public. After Pushpa joined the family, Daulatram had begun exercising some restraint in his conduct towards his wife. But now that they were involved in protecting Adhir from harm, they had opened a joint front against her for they thought that it was she who was driving him to despair. Shakuntala had also found some relief from her husband's habit of ordering her about all the time, not even fetching a glass of water for himself. Even now Daulatram avoided the inner room while Pushpa was there. He shot his barbs from the outer room.

For three days now they had been talking endlessly of the pending enquiry. Adhirath had neither taken Pushpa with him to the lawyer, nor told her or anyone what advice the lawyer had given him.

Pushpa had prepared the file he had taken to Grover. Having seen the photocopy of the daily diary in the file Adhirath said, 'Did I get this when I was suspended? How strange. I had completely forgotten all about it.'

'I got it. You remember Sunita? Sunita Kataria? She used to be with me in the Helpline. Now she is posted here in the thana. I asked her to get it for me. They would have given it to you had you gone and asked for it.' Adhirath fell silent.

But Daulatram had blessed her from the outer room, 'Jeeti raho, beti, live long.' For the first time in his life, he had addressed her as daughter. After the day when she had threatened to leave with her son, Daulatram held his tongue, holding it between his teeth firmly. It was very stressful for him. When Bhikulal called that day to say that there was a strong possibility of Pushpa being promoted, he could no longer hold back.

'God alone knows what is going to happen. My son is proving lucky for his wife. Ever since she has stepped into this house, she has only brought him bad luck.'

'A woman gets her husband's destiny with her own,' Shakuntala jumped in to berate her daughter-in-law. 'There are some who simply erase all the happiness in their husband's lives the moment they tie the knot.'

'This is how it is nowadays. A woman will have her own job, her own bank account. Naturally, she will think only of her own career. Those days are gone when women used to hold their heads high only because their husbands held some high position. They used to be proud on their husband's behalf.'

'That is true,' said Shakuntala. 'Those were days when the wife of a doctor was known as doctorni and the wife of a thanedar was called thanedarni. Now bahu will herself be a thanedarni.'

Both were sitting in the outer room talking in loud voices to ensure that Pushpa heard every word. Then a tempo arrived across the lane and began unloading pipes and bags of rivets on the ground. Shakuntala went in to chop vegetables and Pushpa ran upstairs. A while later, she came down carrying piles of washed and folded clothes.

'Has he told you what the lawyer said?' asked Daulatram.

'No,' said Pushpa shortly.

'Arre, what will he tell her,' Shakuntala weighed in. 'It is because of this ill-omened woman that he does not even stay home nowadays. God knows where all he goes. She never has a good word for him. On top of it threatens to leave him. Who will live with such a grumpy woman?'

Shakuntala was waving a small kitchen knife in the direction of Pushpa. Her voice kept rising with every word. Something in Daulatram snapped. He slapped his wife in the face. Exactly at that moment Varun came in waving his cricket bat, saw what had happened and stopped dead. Pushpa ran to him and hugging him close, coaxed him upstairs. Downstairs they heard screams for a long while. That night Adhirath came home not as late as his habit had been in the last few days. His mother was lying on the cot her face buried in her aanchal. Bapu was spread-eagled on the sofa, one leg off it. The door was open. It was obvious that Pushpa was upstairs. He served himself some cold food and took it upstairs. Pushpa did not say a word to him.

Before leaving for the office, Pushpa handed two hundred-rupee notes to her mother-in-law. Daulatram was reading the paper in the sitting room as if nothing untoward had happened. But Shakuntala's eyes were red, her head bowed. Pushpa placed a hand on her shoulder.

'Ammaji, I never interfere between you two. I request you, you too don't keep commenting on us, please. But tell me, is it not better than getting slapped around...' she let the rest hang in the air. What was the point of advising her in this age?

The mother-in-law shook off her daughter-in-law's hand rudely. Her sympathy smelt of humiliation.

Adhirath arrived downstairs. Daulatram ordered from his sofa, 'Make some tea.'

'What am I hearing?' Adhirath asked. 'Did you hit Amma again?'

'I hit my own wife. Had you learnt to be a man, she would not be hissing at you. Threatens to go away. Standing behind the man is...'

'Do you know Varun saw you do it? What impact will it have on him? You don't like anyone in this house, not Amma, not Pushpa, not me, then get out. Leave. Go where you want to. See if anyone prevents you from leaving.'

'So you have filled his ears nicely?' said Shakuntala to her bahu inside and threw the hundred rupee notes back at her. Pushpa picked them up and left.

'You people have to create such a dust-up all the time, nobody cares what is to happen to me,' said Adhirath. Outside the tempo began to honk. Pushing open the screen door Adhirath strode to the tempo, yanked open its door, pulled out the driver and gave him two tight slaps. 'Saale, you are honking while you are parked here, you bastard? Is it a harmonium that you are fingering it all the time? Running an illegal business in residential area and creating a ruckus all the time. Making life hell for others. I will get your license cancelled, do you hear me?'

The driver was not one to be cowed. He took a pocket full of notes to hand over to the thana every month. Everybody in the neighbourhood knew that the inspector was 'suspend' from his job. When he was posted in the thana, this very driver used to salute Adhirath whenever he saw him and used to take Varun out for a spin in his tempo now and then.

'What will you do?' he now retorted. 'Do what you want. Do you feed me that you raise your hand?'

All the workers had quit loading and were enjoying the fight.

The wife of the tent house owner ran downstairs from her flat and said, 'Arre bhaiyya, come on, spit out your anger, listen to your bhabhi, please, come in,' and pulling Adhir by his arm took him inside his house. Daulatram kept sitting on the sofa. Shakuntala was emerging from the inner room with two cups of tea. Noticing her red rimmed eyes, the neighbour asked after her health and being told that she had a massive headache promised to send some food over and told her that eucalyptus oil works wonders with headache.

Adhirath disentangled his arm and went upstairs. He wanted to get away. He knew he had been running away the whole week. He had spent a fortune on petrol he could ill afford. His job was in danger. Surely this was the time for a family truce? But Pushpa wouldn't bend her stiff spine at all and his father would never learn to behave. He wanted to go somewhere far away. Wear the robes of a sadhu. Go to the hills and become a sanyasi and live in a charas and bhang-induced fog. Only then would he be able to forget all this, get rid of all maya; but the sadhus he saw on TV all seemed to be drowning in maya.

Half an hour later he had left the house, his feet heavy, his stomach and his pockets nearly empty. His mother did not try to stop him.

By a strange coincidence, he spotted Saroj at a red light. He lifted his hands in a namaste from a distance. She threw him a wide smile, even her eyes smiled, and twisting her upturned palm made a gesture asking him where he was headed. Why not go sit under the dome? He followed her car on his bike. When she got down he saw that she was wearing trousers today, white trousers with a white top with fine chikan embroidery. She had the same kangans on her wrists. But today she also had a piece in the same whitish metal around her throat, a thick supple chain like a snake coiled around a stem. Looked like silver but it glowed, it did not look oxidized like old silver. Can't be silver, Adhirath thought.

'Please don't mind, but what you wear, is it silver?' he asked.

Saroj laughed. 'Platinum. Come in, come in. Do you want to search the bedroom again?'

'That can wait,' said Adhir. 'There is a riddle. I want you to solve it for me.'

'Shall we solve it after breakfast?' Saroj said. 'I am hungry today. I've just returned from Hauz Khas. Mamaji fell ill. We were there last night. I always have my breakfast at home.'

And so it was that Adhirath had a sumptuous breakfast in the dining room beyond the dome, at a long glass-topped dining table: curried potatoes, pumpkin sabzi tempered with fenugreek seeds, pooris, dry mango pickle, fried green chillies and yogurt.

'Were you headed this way or did you come only because I saw you?'

Where had he been headed? He did not know.

'Why? Did you want me to come?' he asked.

A smile began to form and vanished before her lips moved.

'I thought maybe you were coming here. Yesterday you went to the farm, so I thought you would come to search the house again.'

'Did Parduman tell you he was going there? He has been living there.'

'He never reported for work after Holi. He called. Said that some policeman has asked for twenty lakhs and if we don't pay up they will accuse Udairaj of having murdered the woman. He said that he went to the farm with Udai and is still there.'

Twenty lakhs!

'You gave the money?'

'Why would I give the money?' said Saroj, laughing this time. She rose and led the way to the small sitting room. Tea arrived.

'What happened to your husband's uncle?' Adhirath asked.

'What happens to old people,' said Saroj. 'He has been left alone. Five sons and daughters, ten-eleven grandchildren, none of them here. Lives in a big, old big house. Most of the rooms are locked. He has diabetes but is very fond of sweets. Sometimes he drinks a lot too. Then he falls sick and dials our number. I went yesterday. Mamaji was perched in the verandah. The moment he saw me get out of the car he began to say, Parduman is very bad, he has been driving my car around the whole day, who knows where he took it. Check the meter, see how many kilometres he has clocked. Kept saying it repeatedly. If the car is not standing right in front of the house, old people begin to feel very insecure.'

'What happened? The car was parked elsewhere?'

'In Hauz Khas? Parking elsewhere? Impossible. People put potted plants in their parking space when they take the car out. Car out, pots in. When you come back, the servant will spend ten minutes removing the pots. It's a lot of work but they seem to think it's worth it.'

'Then?' Adhirath began to get the feeling she was giving him some kind of clue.

'He was here on that day, the day of Holi. Mamaji was here. He returned in our car. His driver had left the car here and gone away. Nobody called the driver to ask him to take back the car.'

'So Parduman took the car back?'

'That I don't know. But the next day too Mamaji's car did

not get back to his house. It was taken there only the day after, that too in the afternoon. A driver from our factory took it there. Must have been parked there somewhere, on the roadside. Let it go. Old people keep worrying about such things. Do you have to go somewhere?'

Adhirath had been watching her closely. Why had it not occurred to him to ask how Mamaji had got here in the first place and if he arrived in his car, what happened to it?

'What kind of car is it?' Adhirath asked.

'Whose? Mamaji's? An old car. Esteem. Black Esteem. He won't buy a new one. Says nobody steals an old car, it is safe.'

'Where is Udairaj?'

'Must be asleep upstairs. The Holi hangover seems to have lasted a few days. He keeps to his bed. One day he went to the thana to get his statement recorded. After that, even his visits to the club have gone down. Yesterday, he went to see Mamaji. They are quite fond of each other. But he returned in the evening.'

'What was he wearing on that day, the day of Holi? What colour were his clothes?' asked Adhirath.

'White kurta. They always wear white. I had told you the first day you came, that it is the tradition in their family. The colours of Holi look good only on white,' Saroj said, now looking at Adhirath carefully.

'And in the morning? Next day? What was he wearing when he opened the door?'

'He was in a kurta. In a yellow kurta,' said Saroj. 'White pajama.'

'He remembered to change his kurta even when he was so drunk?'

Saroj kept quiet.

'Was he wearing the same buttons?' Adhirath asked, his eyes on hers.

Saroj only shook her head slightly.

'Your farmhouse is very beautiful. Parduman told me how much effort you put in to decorate it.'

'What is the use? I cannot spend a single night there. A woman has to first fulfil all the needs of the man,' she said expressionlessly and stood up.

'Is it possible to talk to Udairaj-ji?'

Saroj nodded and went upstairs to check but Udairaj entered the sitting room from some back room and was taken aback to see Adhirath there.

'Please sit down. I had come to talk to you only,' Adhirath said as he saw Saroj arrive at the door of the room.

She came in. 'How are you feeling?' she asked her husband.

Adhirath felt uneasy. There was hardly any affection in her voice, it did not even seem like a question asked for the sake of formality, but as if there was some hidden sign in it, a warning.

Turning to Adhir she said, 'He has become very quiet. Is it necessary to talk to him? I think I should take him to a doctor.'

Udairaj looked irritated. He sat down on a chair and placed his feet onto the table in front of him. The nails of his toes looked well-tended. He began to wiggle them rhythmically.

'Ask,' Udairaj turned to Adhir.

'On the night of Holi, what time did Parduman return?'

'How do I know? I was asleep. When I got up in the morning, the car was not here.'

'He has changed his statement twice.'

'Ask him,' Udairaj shrugged.

'He says that night he took that woman to the farm. You also went there. We also found one of your buttons on the farm.'

Udairaj smirked. 'It is our farm. May have fallen there some time.'

'I never said it was fallen somewhere,' Adhirath interjected immediately.

'Why else would you ask? You wouldn't interrogate me if you had found it in a drawer.'

The man was truly sharp. Or he had rehearsed his answers many times.

'But you did go to the farm that night? Where did you park the Esteem? At the turning of the Chhatarpur Bazaar?'

Udairaj glanced at Saroj and then turned narrowed eyes on Adhiraj.

'So you got the news about the Esteem? My wife is a good detective. You should take her on as your assistant.'

Udairaj studied Adhirath's face. Adhir's hair was now crew cut just like that of cops.

'Did Parduman tell you what he told me yesterday?' Adhirath asked him to throw him off guard.

This time Udairaj surprised Adhirath.

'You want to know the truth? I will tell you the truth. As it is, the whole matter is like a burden on my chest. I can't sleep properly. Saroj, get me a drink please.'

Saroj got up, looking a bit unsettled. She returned bearing a tall glass on a tray. Udairaj took a sip and said, 'No vodka? This seems to be all water. Anyway, it will do.'

'Yes, I went there. For Basanti. Or whatever her name was. I was carrying on with her,' he sighed. 'Her expectations had gone up too much. She wanted rubies and diamonds. Of course, she could not have dreamed that I would marry her, but she had got used to luxury. I had given her some jewellery, clothes. Some cash also. But she always was asking for more. Began to say buy me a flat. I would have. What is thirty-thirty-five lakhs for me? But the factory closed down. The workers filed many cases against us. Whether there is work or not, those workers, they wanted their salaries, their severance pay and what not. We had not paid their wages for four months. We were making losses. There was no work in the factory, they sat idle so why would we pay them, but can you talk sense to the working classes? They want compensation. They say it was not their fault that there was no work. They said they had reported regularly on time for work. Anyway, they filed cases and we shall see when it is decided. I don't know how much the lawyers will bleed us till then. I was under too much stress. At that very time that woman also began to demand, a lot more. I told Parduman that he was the reason I had met her so he should deal with her. But he was busy making money for himself.'

After a brief silence, he continued. 'She,' Udairaj pointed a finger at Saroj and said, 'had really spoilt him. She got him as part of her dowry. Earlier he used to work for her aunt, her mother's sister. His father was their domestic help. When this fellow got trained as a driver they hung him round our neck like a necklace given in dowry. He is good as a driver. But she depended a lot on him. Could not do without him. Going to the parlour? Parduman must take her. Blouses from the tailor? He will do it. Have to buy stones for the house? He will take Bahuji to the place. Which driver does not steal money given for fuel? You send him to the workshop, he will pocket some money. Then he began to loot us in the name of pesticides, fertilizers, daily wage labourers on the farm. I did not bother in the beginning. We had enough. But when foreign companies pitched their tents here, we domestic manufacturers began to suffer; then every small expense began to matter. I thought: let me sell the farm. At one go we will be rid of all our problems. That is why I went there one afternoon.'

'Really?' asked Adhirath. His voice dripped with sarcasm.

'Ok, that was much before the crisis set in. I went there, for whatever reason. What do I find? The man is sprawled in our bedroom with that woman. But the noose he had put around his neck was very colourful. She was young. And to tell you the truth she had a lot of practice in pleasing men. She knew a lot of ways to do the same thing. The only problem was she talked too much. As long as she kept her mouth shut nobody could guess she was a low-class woman from a village. She looked upper class. Later, I also got her the right clothes. But the moment she opened her mouth, it was clear what she was. She insisted on speaking English and that gave the game away. Bad pronunciation. Broken English. Then she began to steal. Once I spent the night there. Took off all four buttons of the kurta and put them on the bedside table. In the morning, there were only three. A gold button studded with a diamond. I searched everywhere, looked under the bed, behind the table. Nowhere. She began to show me her purse to prove she had not taken it. I had to hold my peace. I told him, that Parduman, to make her understand that I had had enough of her.

'He is also a snake of the first water. The thing with old servants is that they know everything about the family. On top of it, he was a favourite with Bahuji. Look at his gumption. He brought that woman here. Not once but two or three times. He would ask Papaji to get her some work, or ask my wife to get her makeup done by her. He told them some other name but what did that matter? Anyway, it was clear, he wanted to scare me. I told him, go tell Saroj whatever you want to tell. Why should I be afraid? I am a man. Women came to me in droves. What will happen? At the most she will divorce me. Let her.'

Adhirath was impressed by Saroj's complete indifference to all these revelations. There was no revulsion on her face nor any anger. Udairaj had emptied his glass. He went in to fix another drink. Adhirath felt that his frank admission of his two-timing his wife had disturbed him more than it affected Saroj. Could it be that being ill-treated by him for years and suffering all kinds of humiliation, this woman was trying to dump a murder case on him as a form of revenge? The job of the police is not a good one. They have to keep fighting off the chill of reality to keep their own relationships warm. Pushpa would leave him if the tension got too much, there were no diamond bracelets or acres of land to hold her back.

Udairaj returned. He asked Adhirath if he could get him one too. Adhirath refused. Udairaj shrugged and began to sip at his drink, looking straight at his wife.

'Then they changed tactics. Told me she was pregnant. Now she became very bold. Now she wanted a house for herself. How would I know whether she was pregnant or fibbing? I could not take her to a doctor. I would now have to keep her hanging around for at least six months, only then I would know whether it was the truth or not. I thought, let me have fun for a few more months. I even told her that this is an obstacle to our enjoyment so she should get rid of it. Get an abortion. But she did not agree. Began to behave like she was Mother India or something. Said she could not take a life! What is the fault of the child? Why should it be killed? It is a sin! She had been sleeping with who knows how many people, umpteen, I am sure, and that in her book was not a sin, this was.

'I called Parduman and told him to get rid of her. I meant he should pay her off or hand her over to someone else. Anything, but I did not want anything more to do with her. He misunderstood me.

'One day he came to me and said it would cost five lakhs. I asked him what he meant. He says to me, she won't return, ever, to harass me. I said will she go away for good for such an amount, considering what she had been asking for. He said yes. I bargained a bit and we settled on four lakhs. He said to me to be nice to her for some days, after that he would take care of her. So, I began to mollycoddle her. "Will it look nice that your second child will grow up in a dark room, go to a government school," she would ask me. So I said sarcastically, "Why would he be born in a government hospital? Why would he live in poverty? Start living here, on the farm! I will buy you some land nearby." She took me literally. Told the manager that she would soon be his boss, she would have her own farm nearby. She simply did not know where she belonged. However pretty a sandal is, nobody turns it into a necklace.

'Parduman told me that on the day of Holi, she would leave town for good. That day we had a big party here. I had gone upstairs and was standing in the balcony. I don't know why I had gone there. He was carrying a crate of Coca-Cola to the basement. His mobile must have rung. He placed the crate on the ground and took the call. It was very noisy down there, loud music was playing so he walked away from the entry to the basement and began to talk. He had to raise his voice to be heard. I heard him too. He was saying, "Get to the farm, I will come there. Now it is going to be your property anyway." Then, after a while he said, "Okay, I will pick you up from the bazaar at the usual place." I got suspicious. He had told me she would go away for good that day and there he was asking her to come to the farm. I could have collared him then and there but I thought it will better to catch them red handed.'

'So when you said, "get rid of her," you meant driving her

out of town? Nothing else?' Adhirath asked. He was tempted to down a glass of vodka.

Udairaj spoke without hesitation. 'What else could it mean? In the factory, we use this phrase. If a worker starts acting over-smart, we say, "Get rid of him, set him right". We don't go killing them.'

'And on the night of Holi?'

'I said I was feeling ill. Bolted the door from inside. Only after Mamaji left did I venture out. Our room has a latch key, and does not open without a key. I took the key and locked the door. Saroj did not have the key to it. I had left the mobile phone inside the room. I crept downstairs from the other staircase. The stairs lead to a door outside on the other side of the house that is generally left open so that if I return late nobody has to get up to let me in. I had taken the keys to Mamaji's car while I had been chatting with him. That was easy. My clothes were painted in many colours. There was no need to change them. It was a good camouflage. Had anybody who knew me even ran into me, he would have thought I was drunk and had not had a bath. After all, it was Holi! I put on a cap and got into the Esteem. Nobody seems to have seen me. Everybody was either drunk or tired or out for the count. The servants were sleeping inside. The children, my son and his cousins and friends, were in the basement. But even then I could have been spotted. I was lucky. Nobody did.'

Udairaj fell silent. Saroj turned her face towards Adhirath. A neutral, expressionless face. She was so still that even the platinum snake around her throat did not stir.

'Why did you not take the car up to the farm?'

'It occurred to me on the way. They would be warned by the headlights of the car. That is why I left the car at the turning of the village. Where the main road turns into Jhandapur. A little distance away from the station. It was a moonlit night. It did not take me long to get to the farm.'

'He walks at least five kilometres a day. Goes to the gym. He keeps fit,' said Saroj speaking for the first time. Both looked at her.

What was it in her tone? Praise for her good-looking husband? Envy, for having lost such a fit body to a spring flower, a Basanti? Or was it a simple confirmation of his ability to walk for such a long distance in order to commit a murder?

'I saw my car on the way, under those trees. I saw it only because a train passed by and picked it up in its headlights. I don't know whether villagers go to sleep early or just shut themselves inside their houses soon. It could also have been because of Holi. All was eerily quiet. There are so many trees there. No dearth of shadows. I kept to the shadows. I had just reached the gate when what do I see, but two men getting out, in dhotis. Must have been villagers. I was dumbstruck. I stopped under a tree. They left and when I reached the gate, Parduman was standing there, near the verandah. No sign of Cheti. Of course, I had given him permission to spend the night away from the house. That is when I heard her screams. She came out screaming. That Basanti. She was saying I am not a randi. That is when I understood what had been going on. That bastard had found a good way to make money. I asked him what he was up to. "I asked you to get rid of her and here you are turning the farmhouse into a fancy brothel," is what I said to him. She heard me all right. So, she began to scream even more loudly to say what did he think she was, some whore or what, that whoever wants to climbs on to her can do so, and anybody who wants can...I can't even say those words. Her language was such that a decent man would need to wash his ears out afterwards. It had been a terrible mistake, getting involved with her. I understood exactly what had happened. First this Parduman, then those two men, they had done whatever they wanted to with her. I don't know how many times this had happened before. And whose baby she was carrying. They were trying to hold me responsible, both of them.'

When Udairaj saw Adhirath was about to say something, he raised his hands and said, 'Yes, it could well have been mine. Even then. They could do whatever they wanted to, but not in my house. I told Parduman that much. I was so furious, I felt such deep hatred for him and his activities that I even forgot to take the keys to my car from him. I gave that Basanti a good hard kick. She fell down there in the garden. I told Parduman that the sheets of the bed, everything should be changed. I walked away fast, walked up to Mamaji's car and came home.'

'Why Mamaji's car?'

'I had forgotten to take the keys to my own car from the driver.'

He paused. He was panting a little now. 'I went straight up to my room. When Papaji woke me up in the morning I had a heavy head.'

'So you are saying that Parduman alone killed her, having taken money to give to her.'

'You can assume whatever you want to.'

'That cut she was given. It was done by a very sharp knife. Where did that knife come from?'

'Arre, that knife used to be on the farm. You know butchers have that kind of knife. That Parduman had become quite an expert at wielding it. He used to kill hares on the farm, could slit their abdomens with a straight cut. Once a kid neelgai ventured into the farm and could not get out. It was running helter skelter. Nachchatar and Parduman lassoed it with a rope. Then they tied him to a tree. Parduman slit its throat in one go. That way the fellow is very skilled. Truly, I can't tell you how delicious that meat was. All the servants on the farm ate it, there was so much. Some villagers also got their share. Parduman says neelgai are not cows, they are a kind of deer. Even then I felt very bad afterwards. I made penance. Had Satyanarayan katha. Had I given a gold cow to panditji everybody would have suspected me of committing a sin. So I got a gold coin made with a cow etched on one side and the goddess Lakshmi on the other. That must have been two, no, three years ago'

'Where did you change your clothes?' Adhirath asked.

'Which clothes?'

'The ones you wore on Holi? The ones you went to the farm in? They must have got stained with blood. You wore something you had kept on the farm? The yellow kurta was there, was it not?'

Udairaj laughed. 'Prove it. I will accept the superiority of your intellect if you do so.'

Saroj looked up startled.

'You will be able to prove, won't you, that you had lost the button a long time ago?'

'You prove that you found it lying around.'

'One last question.' Adhirath leaned towards him. 'Why did you not tell us all this in the club? Then you maintained that you were home the whole night.'

Udairaj looked at Saroj, then at Adhirath. Emptying his glass, he said, 'I have been running a business. My lawyers have always told me to never make any statement without first getting it cleared by them.'

'Oh, a lawyer is advising you now!' said Adhirath.

'Yes, and he says that I should tell the whole truth. He says, "When you have committed no crime why should you be afraid? Yes, you have been unfair to Saroj, there you are culpable." And he's right. That is what has been weighing on me. I am glad I had this talk with you. Saroj has also heard everything. Otherwise, I don't know how I would have been able to tell her.'

A faint smile began to play on his lips. Adhirath felt that Udairaj was throwing him a challenge. He got up to leave. Udairaj saw him to the door.

Adhirath kicked his mobike and was about to get onto it when his phone rang. Dalchand. Till now his family had not bothered to find out where he was. A deep disappointment told him however much he fought with them, it hurt to think that nobody there needed him. He wanted to disconnect the call. Then it occurred to him that if poverty stricken Dalchand was calling him, he definitely must have something to say. He let the phone ring till it went silent. Then he called back.

'I was on the motorcycle,' he said. 'By the time I stopped, it got disconnected. Anything important?'

'They had called me, Janaab. Kashyap sahib did the enquiry,' Dalchand said.

'Okay,' he managed.

'I told them that I had to go on the round of Bargadiya Gali with you but at the last minute I was told to go to court so I could not go. That the round was part of our daily plan. That is all I could do, Janaab. I even told them that even when we make rounds, people do not notice or lie about our ever having come there. They are determined not to tell the truth when it comes to the police, what can we do? They never tell the truth about the police and never tell the truth to the police. So I said you must have definitely gone to Bargadiya Gali. That is what I said to them. I said all this on my own. They did not ask me.'

Adhirath was moved to tears. He had been abusing this man just a moment earlier. What could Dalchand do? His neck was in the noose. If he were convicted he would go in for at least ten or twenty years. It is not easy, there are many enemies of policemen inside the prison, and anyone can use a blade on your jugular.

'Dalchand, listen to me, man, those who are our own remain our own. Yaar you have done a lot for me, a lot. I will never forget this. Truly. Never will I forget this favour. I had not thought you would do this much.' He had to stop for there was a catch in his throat.

11

The aroma of spices floated out of the screen door. There was a time when the house used to be redolent with such smells. The moment he smelt these spices, he would think that there was going to be a party that night because some relatives or Bapu's colleagues have come over. There would be meat in a rich curry with potatoes and hot phulkas would be served with it. The memory of those days hit him now. He knew there would be swollen faces inside. Perhaps his sister was here...no, why would she come? She might know that he was going to face an enquiry tomorrow. She would when everything was over and done with.

Varun was in the sitting room eating keema balls with ketchup. Daulatram was breaking open the fried balls and blowing on them to cool them down before placing them back on his plate.

'Tell Bahu that her son is finding the balls very hot, she should fry them a little cold,' said Daulatram.

'Ok, I will wash them in cold water for him,' said Shakuntala.

'Dadaji is joking, don't wash them,' said Varun, squeezing words from his stuffed mouth.

Adhirath was stunned to see such bonhomie at home. Pushpa was frying mince balls in a kadahi, his mother was scooping up the spiced minced meat from the paraat to roll them into small marbles. Why couldn't his home always be like this?

'What happened? Looks like you have been promoted,' said Adhirath.

'Wash your hands, I'll give you some hot ones.' said Pushpa. 'The list of promoted people is ready but not out.'

'Even then news gets out.'

'All this is for you,' said Shakuntala.

In the afternoon, Pushpa had come home early and sat down in front of her father-in-law in the sitting room, something she never did. 'Papaji, you know how bad tomorrow is going to be for him. It will be good if there is less tension at home. If you get some mince from the market, I could make some koftas. You know how much Adhir likes them. I was about to say this to mummy in the morning but well...' she handed over a hundred rupee note to him.

'This won't be enough,' said Daulatram, pulling on a shirt over his banyan. 'I have money. I'll get a whole kilo. Arre can you hear me, wash your face and practice smiling, we are all doing our best for your son only.'

The moment he left, Pushpa said to her mother-in-law, 'Had I been in your place I would have called the Helpline. I am posted there, you know.'

Shakuntala said nothing. However, when Pushpa said, 'Come on, give me some tea,' she turned and said, 'Would you order your mother about? Make your own tea.'

'Yes, I used to order my mum about. The poor thing did not live to see that her daughter had married someone in a higher caste. That too without giving any dowry. Even our Commissioner cannot perform such a great task. But did I get a medal? No way. Had I even got a mother-in-law who was like a mother, I would have been content. Even that is not written in my fate.'

Shauntala was taken aback. All of a sudden Pushpa burst out laughing. 'Let us play act today, Matashree. It is necessary. For your son. Ceasefire!'

Now Adhirath sat down next to Varun and his father gave him a glass of rum. His son thrust half a kofta into his mouth.

'Homework?' asked Adhirath.

Varun looked at his grandfather.

'He will do it. Or else he can have a holiday,' said Daulatram. 'We had been waiting for a long time. Thank God, you came on time. These koftas are best hot.'

After they had polished off the kofta curry with crisp chapattis, Daulatram asked him, 'What did the lawyer say?'

Adhirath told him.

'He charged twenty-five thousand to say that much?' Daulatram could barely get the words out. He was outraged and he was drunk.

Adhirath went upstairs. Varun had gone to bed with his grandmother where she had been telling him a story. Adhirath used to carry him upstairs when he did this but today he did not. Today he wanted a carefree night with his wife. He knew after tomorrow the curtain would fall on this happy scene and the dust of reality would cover it once again.

Late at night, he recalled what Udairaj had told him at the door. Saroj had not accompanied them.

'You can get any number of call girls, why then...?' he let the question hang.

'That is true. I can find plenty of women. Even so, I got entangled with this gutter mouth. And then I stayed entangled.'

'Why? What did she do that others could not?' Adhirath was thinking of Saroj's simplicity and composure.

Udairaj laughed silently. 'I can't even begin telling you what a catch she was. Completely free of inhibitions. At times she would dance in the nude, forgetting everything, even herself. Frankly, there was not one fantasy of a male she could not play out. She was so supple, so flexible...you have seen yogis or those girls who can bend anything any which way? Hands this way, legs that way. So flexible...had my wife been like this I would have dumped her the next day, sent her back to her parents, and wanted to know where she learnt all this. It seems Parduman was angry with me. After coming to my bed why would she or anyone go to his cot? But a harlot she was. Some are high class, some are low class, but in bed she was truly in a class of her own.'

'Pushpi, can you dance?' Adhirath asked her.

'Of course. I have danced at so many weddings. Why?'

Adhirath covered her unclad breasts with an arm and said, 'I thought you could dance for me, as you are. Without your clothes. Only for me.'

'Are you mad?' Pushpa asked pulling him over.

His steps began to slow outside the building. It was not as if he had not been here. They all had to visit this place off and on. Then he used to be in uniform. People used to smile at him, they would greet him, he would climb the stairs with confidence. This was the same building, the same metal detector, the same officers. But today he was not in uniform. Today his steps faltered. He crossed the metal detector quietly. By the time he reached the Deputy Commissioner's office, every room seemed unfamiliar. It felt like he had no friends here. He could only see walls. Among the men seated on chairs behind these alien walls was not one person who would listen to him, understand him, show him a way to get out of this mess, hold his hand and walk with him.

He began to find his file heavy. A few sheets of paper had the strength to change the direction of his life. They could change the future of his son. To decide what he would find on his plate and what he would not. Whatever he had done until today, whatever he had earned, everything could be buried under these few sheets. The words on these papers outweighed his standing, his record.

By the time he reached the single-member enquiry committee of Shriman Dilip Singh Kashyap, his alienation was so complete that he felt he was not inside his body at all. He felt as if a stranger were sitting there and what happened to that stranger did not matter to him.

'Never tell them the truth,' Nitesh had said.

'Deny everything,' Pushpa had said.

'Let them prove their case,' the lawyer who charged him twenty-five grand had said.

'Tell them only what is necessary. Your first duty is to yourself, to protect yourself,' his mind said wearily.

'That day you were on leave?'

'No sir. I was before that day. I had taken a week's leave. I joined early.'

'Why?' the DCP asked.

'I thought I would save the leave for later.'

'Is this your writing?'

The Daily Diary was placed before him.

'Looks like it, sir.'

'Is it your handwriting or not?'

Whom could he blame? That SHO was of equal rank, but

he had gone to court early in the morning. All the others were subordinates. Whom would he sacrifice? He could deny it was his writing but then whom would he point his finger at?

'Is it your writing or not?'

Finally: 'It is, sir, it is.'

Now the matter had been decided. What need for more questions? What use? He had dug his own grave. Then why ask more questions? All they had to do was throw mud on him. He laughed.

'Why did you mark your attendance like this squeezed between two names?'

Adhirath looked at the face of the DCP. There was not a single line of sympathy anywhere on that face. A callous face, expressionless.

'I had forgotten to mark my attendance. I did that later.'

'Your application for leave? Did you take it out of the file?'

Adhirath swallowed air. It was bitter.

'Sir, the truth is...'

The DCP's hand came up to stop him.

'I know the facts. I only have to check whatever is on record. Why such a record? I have superiors above me. Complaints can be filed against me also. So let us confine ourselves to these documents. Did you take out the leave application from the file?'

'Yes, I did.'

'Why?'

'I thought I would write an application for only three days' leave and put it in there. Those who had sanctioned my leave would understand my compulsions.'

'Ok. That is enough. Now my next question.'

'Sir, how can that be enough? My compulsions are the department's compulsions. This, the department will have to understand and acknowledge my compulsions.'

'In this diary is written that you went to the Bargadiya Gali for a round. Dalchand Hawaldar was with you. Did you write this?'

'Yes. I wrote this.' Adhirath recalled that day. How he had rushed to the thana having disengaged Pushpa's fingers from his shirt. How much he had suffered for living close to the thana. Had his house been far away, he would not not been able to reach it so soon. There had been no officer in the police station. And without sparing a moment's thought, he had made all those notations to save Dalchand. He had realized rather late in the day that in this department nobody does anything for anyone else. Those who had handed Dalchand over to the court, despite the detailed plans they had made, why would they let Adhirath go? All of them were busy saving their own uniforms. At a moment's notice, they had announced to the newspapers that they will dismiss the hawaldar who fired the gun. Those who handed him a country made pistol, told him what to do, planned his alibi, none of them had to suffer, nobody touched them, and they were all in the clear, still in their uniforms. What a job! If you show fidelity to the law, people won't be with you. If you exterminate those who make the lives of ordinary citizens hell, the law will not be with you. His eyes grew moist.

The DCP was watching him closely, his pupils narrowed a little. He saw in those eyes, disdain for himself. It jumped up to crawl on his back like a worm. Instantly his spine snapped to attention. He had shaken off the worm. He was free. He had done whatever he had done with full awareness of what he was doing, of his own free will. He would not bow to these slaves of evidence. The truth, subservient only to documentary evidence, was not acceptable to him. From palm leaves to these papers, this system had used documents to invent lies and present them as truth. He had seen himself how easily evidence is created and how easily erased.

'Sir, the truth is that I tried to protect a hawaldar of mine. The truth is I did not hatch any conspiracy. I did not plan anything that happened that day. I only tried to help a subordinate. The truth is whatever Dalchand did, he did not do of his own accord. He said yes, but all "yes-es" are not consent, you know that and I also know that. If you think I am guilty, punish me. I know nobody in Bargadiya Gali saw any police jeep. You have witnesses to tell you that the police did not patrol the place that day. I know. Dalchand also may have told you that he did not go with me on the tour of inspection. I know many people saw Dalchand kill the man. You have witnesses. People saw Satthiya kill so many times but we had no witnesses. Not one. I have nothing more to say to this Enquiry Committee. Thank you.'

Adhirath stood up and walked out.

His back was straight, his step confident.

12

In the evening he called Nitesh. 'Have to meet, you, yaar.'

'Arre, I am here in the neighbourhood. In Preet Vihar. Come over, we can meet here, let us go to Sagar Ratna,' Nitesh said.

Sagar Ratna! Adhir did not have that kind of money. Actually, he had right now, but that was the money Nitesh had lent him. Even otherwise he would hardly allow him to pay the bill. It would be good if he left before Pushpa came home. He took a bus and got down at Lakshmi Nagar. He walked up to the next stop. There was no need to spend another fiver on the ticket. He had been spending too much in the last ten days or so.

He told Nitesh that he had no expectations of justice from the Enquiry Committee.

'Meaning? You didn't deny?'

'I told them the truth. Dalchand is paying the price, I can also do it.'

Nitesh said, 'But they will...'

'Yes, what?'

'Forget it.'

'No, say it. This is a very bad habit you have. Don't begin to say things and then stop. Either you say something and then you say the whole thing or you shut up. That day too you said

Bapu had said something about Pushpa. But you have not told me till now. Today, I ask you in the name of our friendship, what was it? Today I will only get up when you have told me both the things.'

'I was about to say that punishing you would seem like justice to them. What is justice for us is not justice for them.'

'I created evidence. I made false entries. Those are facts. I deserve to be penalized. If I had consulted a lawyer before I did all that, nobody would have been able to touch a hair on my head. Like that loathsome fellow is doing, what's his name, that Udairaj.'

'What is he doing?' asked Nitesh.

'He has consulted a lawyer and prepared his defence. He is a murderer. He and Parduman, they both got together to kill that woman.'

'How can that be possible? Where is the proof?' Nitesh was shaken.

'That button, you know, when Udairaj was strangulating her, it fell there. The threads she wore around her wrist were caught in it.'

'You say anything that enters your head,' said Nitesh. 'Let us assume it fell there but how can you prove it fell there on that very day? She could have worn those threads earlier. It could be the threads of one of his kurtas.'

Adhirath knew his statement had no weight. The button could have been the one she had stolen earlier. Perhaps she had strung it around her neck and in the struggle, it had fallen off.

'You mean it did not fall off in the room when she was raped and she was struggling so hard, but it fell off outside?'

'The rape happened later. First, she slept with Parduman. She may have taken it off, and she wore it again when she went out...'

'She remembered to put it on even in those conditions?' Nitesh sounded incredulous.

'Why not? She always kept it on her. It was her savings account, what she had earned in her life...'

'Earned? Adhir, you've lost it. She stole it.'

'She took it. It was remuneration for the extreme pleasure she gave that man. He should have given her the diamond himself.'

'Granted. But see how a whore's earnings end in the dust?' said Nitesh. 'Why are you feeling so sympathetic to her?'

'Because we are all whores!' said Adhirath, teeth clenched. 'We take things from the maalkhana, make false entries in registers. We are unscrupulous. Do we sell our consciences every day or not?'

Nitesh was stupefied. After a while he said, 'Yaar, I know you are under much strain. Come on spit out your anger. How does it matter to me? If Udairaj is a murderer, he is. I only need proof that he is.'

'You find the proof. It is your job. I found it. But you will not accept the statement he made to me. Come, make me a witness. He says he asked Parduman to get rid of the woman. He paid him four lakhs. She was going to give birth to his child. Do you think in four lakhs she would have given up her claims? She would have asked for a share in his property. You searched the farmhouse. Did you know Parduman was there even at that time? That is where he had been hiding. Why did you not apprehend him? Because you could not find him. Did you find the murder weapon? You did not. These people are very shrewd. Very, very clever.'

'Listen, don't get angry, man. Such cases will happen every day. And yes, I think you told me that his wife had said that the button was lost before Holi...the murder did not take place before Holi. But we have caught hold of Parduman. We have found three witnesses. They had seen him that night. Parking his car under some trees and hotfooting it to the farm.'

'When did all this happen?'

'Today, just a couple of hours ago. Actually, yesterday morning, a man called. He was saying he had some information and was very scared, he too could be killed. So I went to Jhandapur village. The three boys are from that village. That four lakhs you are talking about, we did not find them on Parduman. We conducted a raid on his house. He was absconding. We spread a net then and got him. It is true that this crorepati was carrying on with that woman. But why would he get her killed? They can buy any number of such women. Anyway, Udairaj helped me get hold of Parduman. We traced his phone to the farm but we could not find him there. Then Udairaj helped us trace him. He is the one who called him and said that he had arranged some place for him to run away to.'

'You did a good job, boss,' said Adhirath.

'Udairaj asked him to come to the Interstate Bus Stop near Kashmiri Gate. He himself went there in a taxi.'

'Why, what did he say, "It does not matter that you are a murderer, I like you so much I am going to help you"?' Adhirath sniggered.

'Yaar, you are misreading the whole thing. What do you mean I found nothing in the farmhouse? I found that girl's clothes. And Parduman's clothes too. It was clear they were used to staying there. Both of them. Come, let us go. It is getting late,' Nitesh motioned to the waiter to get them their bill.

The manager came to their table. 'Sir, why do you have to pay for such a little snack? I am so grateful you gave us a chance to serve you.'

'When we take a favour, it will be a big one. We don't take small bribes,' said Nitesh and went to the counter to pay.

The full moon of Holi had shrunk to a crescent. The market glittered with lamps and neon signs. A flood of cars washed over the roads. Everything seemed unchanged. Nitesh cranked open the jeep door and said, 'Let us meet in a day or two.'

'Wait,' said Adhir. 'You had to tell me that other thing also. What my father said about Pushpa.'

'I have forgotten,' said Nitesh. He had climbed in and was about to shut the door. Adhirath opened the back door and got in. With the closing of the door, he shut out some of the clamour from outside but the hum of noise filtered in even through metal and glass doors. No escape, his mind said as he tried to concentrate on compelling Nitesh to tell him what he had once begun to tell. Nitesh motioned to the hawaldar on the driving seat and he got out.

Turning towards Adhirath, he said, 'You should not insist.' Adhirath kept staring at him.

Unsettled, Nitesh continued, 'You know what a good trick I played? I got Udairaj to tell Parduman that the police was suspecting both of them. He said he was going to stay with his brother for some time and there he would think of some way to deal with this. Nobody would suspect them of having absconded because one can always go to one's brother's place, especially at festival times. They could even run away to Nepal from there. He asked Parduman to reach the bus station. Said he would bring the car. Then Parduman could drive him up to his brother's house. Parduman had left the farm and was hiding at some other friend's house. We came in two jeeps, a full team. Udairaj went in a taxi. Parduman came to the bus station and we grabbed him there, along with his clothes. But those lakhs of rupees were not on him. A man who is about to abscond would carry all that dosh with him, wouldn't he? Wasn't that a good trick? I sent him with my ASI to the thana and came here with Udairaj. That is when you called.'

'Now tell me what he said about Pushpa.'

'If you insist. Uncle said to me that women of her caste can't be trusted. They meet a lot of people. Only he did not say "meet" he said something obscene. He said they don't belong to one person, they have many relationships. Who knows whether Pushpa was also born of her father or not.'

Adhirath got out of the car.

Pushpa was sweeping the place early in the morning. She did it sometimes on holidays, swept every corner clean. Took down the pants and shirts hanging from brackets behind the doors, wiped the doors clean, demolished the houses of insects built in crevices, moved all the chairs, stools, and tables and readied the room so that it might welcome a fresh film of dust. She pulled out the trunk from under the bed.

'Why don't you return it?' she asked as she swept its dusty top with her broom.

He should return it. The woman whose name he had used to get it here, she was the only one with any rights to it.

'See what beautiful clothes she had,' Adhirath said opening the trunk.

Pushpa wore khaki most of the time and at home she wore faded old clothes. She had practically forgotten what vibrant colours look like. When did she ever get the opportunity or time to wear them? She could not wear ironed and starched clothes to cook and swab the house. But the moment she saw the brilliant colours of the lehenga, her eyes began to sparkle. How keenly she had wanted to wear a lehenga for her wedding but both their families had been so opposed to their marriage that nothing she wanted could be done.

It was not clear whether the blue had overlaid the red or the red was printed above the blue but both the colours were a swirl in the lehanga. It had a broad golden border. The black braided tape at the waist had a shower of golden specks. Such tapes are not meant to be hidden inside the petticoat but to be displayed proudly, to be slung from the waist and spun around with gyrations. To keep them hanging, there are intricately designed weights. Only a woman would have taken that spangled weight of beads in her hand to admire its bell shape and the border of tiny sequins hanging from it. Dazzling rays lit up the dusty room.

'What is this?' asked Pushpa. Even in that mass of rolled gold trinkets, she noticed a real gold disc tied securely with a string to the top of the bell-shaped weight at the bottom of a tape. It was not part of the original braid. It was different, two gold coins joined together with a stem. The larger of the two flashed diamond fire. Deprived of gold and finery, Pushpa had been able to spot the missing button. For a moment, Adhirath saluted the departed Suryabala. She had used the oldest trick in the book: hiding her insurance in plain sight.

Here was the fourth button. That is what Udairaj had said, that he had four buttons. How had he forgotten to ask the industrialist how many buttons he had now? Had Saroj also noticed that two buttons were missing now or was she unaware? So this was the first button he claimed the woman had stolen. The one he had found that day under the bay window, that he had gone wearing to the farmhouse.

'Is it a diamond? It is exactly like the one you got earlier,' she said.

'The one I got earlier belonged to Udairaj. This one belongs to the woman,' he said.

Pushpa caressed the button in her palm. If they had this, they could pay off all the loans, her empty bank account would get back the cash she had withdrawn. She tried to pull the string, but it did not break. She fetched a pair of scissors and cut it. Then she replaced the button in the purse she found in the trunk.

'Take it back. And do it today,' she said picking up her broom. 'One should not tempt the mind.'

'Don't you want the lehenga?' asked Adhirath.

Pushpa threw a startled glance at him. Adhirath's looked almost apologetic. She laughed.

'I can get one made,' she said. 'I have stopped wearing the discards of the dead.'

'I did not mean to...'

'...taunt me about my caste. I know. Had I not known I would have left you a long time back.' She sat down on the floor throwing the broom aside. Adhirath too got down to sit by her side. He pulled out several fashionable clothes from the trunk to show her. She flung them upwards and said, 'Some day we shall be able to afford them. But you know what? Even if I got them and wore them, you would only enjoy pulling them off, wouldn't you?'

The clothes rained down on them but she got out from under them and ran, he ran after her, but where was there to run and play hide and seek? Upstairs, an open terrace. Downstairs are parents. He could slap her there, in public, but he could not kiss her there. If he slapped her in public, his father would pat him on the back, people would praise him for being a man. But if they kissed, they would be called shameless. He could not hug his own wife in the presence of others. What a civilization! All this vigilance trained on love, never aimed at hate.

'Why are people so afraid of love?' Adhirath asked.

'Maybe because love has so much power?' Pushpa nuzzled his arm.

Two hours later he went to meet Saroj. He did not know why but he had this feeling that she was in his camp. She was getting inside the car and stopped when she saw him. She told him she was on her way to Mamaji's.

'Is there anything important?'

'Had to ask something,' said Adhirath in a low voice. 'You told me you had lost a gold button. Your husband had. That is why he wore one button less on the day of Holi. How many did he wear?'

'Three. I told you even earlier,' she replied. Her tone was normal.

'How many buttons do you have now?'

'Will have to check,' said Saroj. 'Since then I have not checked his things. He keeps the keys to his cupboard with him.'

'He did not do so earlier?'

'No, this is new. For some months he has been doing this. But if I ask for the keys he may even give them to me.'

'How long will it take?'

'Well at least till the evening. I am going out now. He is not at home either. If I get back early and he is here, it may happen earlier. I will call you,' Saroj said. 'Is it very important?'

Adhirath sighed. What could be so important now? What

difference would it make now? How would he prove that he found the button in her trunk? He had not found it when he had been looking for it.

'I just wanted to know,' he said.

'Been a long time, Ustad,' said Bharat when he saw him. 'A lot happened behind your back.'

Adhirath said, 'Let's take a look at the farm.'

'And this trunk? You want to leave it here on the bike?'

Bharat picked up the trunk from the back of his bike and placed it inside his room and got onto the bike. Adhirath asked, turning the motorcycle towards the farm, 'What is the news? Will the farm be sold?'

'Doesn't look like it. One day madam came here after you stopped coming. She has given Cheti a raise. Nachchatar has been asked to come check the farm and its work off and on as a part-time supervisor. She will pay him for it.'

This was news for Adhirath. When they reached the farm, Cheti came running to open the gate. A tractor was ploughing the field behind the borderline of trees near the pond. It was now getting to be unpleasantly warm in the city, but here it was still cool and breezy.

'I wanted to see the black partridge,' said Adhirath.

Both sat down on a bench near the neel kamal pond.

'That Parduman was caught,' said Adhirath. 'By now the police may have fished out his clothes and the murder weapon also.'

'I told madam to keep a dog here. At least it would bark if someone came,' Bharat said.

'He did not do it alone,' said Adhir. 'But the rich man will get away.'

'Nothing ever happens to the rich, na?'

Adhirath nodded. Still Bharat looked very happy. 'We were the ones who gathered all the evidence. The police got them only later. Those fellows, they told the police what they saw,' said Bharat. 'Jhandapuriyas are delighted. One of them bought a new mobile phone only yesterday. What a glossy thing it is. Those three got drunk under that same chaukhamba, the day Parduman was caught.'

'Why are the Jhandapuriyas delighted?'

'Where did the murder take place? In Chandola. Who helped the police nab the murderer? Jhandapuriyas. It is something to be proud of.'

'I went to the thana before I came here,' said Adhir. 'Nitesh wasn't there. That is why I managed to talk to Parduman. He is in the lockup. He says three lakh seventy-seven thousand rupees were on him when they nabbed him. Of that, twenty-seven thousand were his own savings. But the police did not show the money in the seizure list. Only two policemen had found the money, Nitesh and an ASI, while the rest were busy elsewhere. Fifty he had already paid the Jhandapuriyas. He said that Udairaj might have paid the Jhandapuriyas more money to rat on him and become witnesses for the prosecution.'

'Damn, that's impressive,' said Bharat.

Cheti brought them tea.

Adhirath told Bharat the story of the diamond-studded button. 'This button I found here was not the one that she had stolen earlier. The one she stole I found in her trunk. This was the one that fell off in the struggle. When Basanti was grappling with Udairaj to get free, it got tangled in the threads she had around her wrist and came off. The threads were still around it when I found it. The buttonhole in his kurta may have a tear. It was a new kurta so the tear can prove a lot of things. Has that kurta been shown in the list of items seized? I wonder.'

'So you found the second button too?' Bharat said looking into Adhir's eyes.

They got up and made two rounds of the little pond. Cheti was running after the tractor shouting some instructions. Perhaps he was telling the driver how much grass had been left behind by his plough.

'We have something to do,' said Adhirath.

'Say.'

'We must go to Amirpur. To meet Basanti...no Suryabala's mother. I had promised to tell her who killed her daughter. Will you come? Have to give her the trunk also.'

'Let us go,' said Bharat.

When they returned the trunk to Ramwati in Amirpur, she said nothing. She did not say that her daughter was a characterless woman and so she had no desire to touch her things. She did not even cry when she saw the colours of the clothes. Adhir had seen both daughters-in-law peering out at them from an inner room. He was sure the young women would start squabbling over the clothes the moment they left.

Ramwati did not offer them tea. She heard him out silently. Adhirath said, 'Ammaji, I am sorry. I could not do much. You must forgive me.'

'A constable had come to tell me that someone called Parduman has been caught. I had not thought you would come, beta. She was my daughter. She was not good and she died like that too, the way she died was also not good. At least she will send one man to the gallows,' said Ramwati almost indifferently.

Suddenly he felt a wave of revulsion sweep over him for Ramwati also. He got up abruptly. When they began to leave, he laid his hands on Ramwati's shoulders and walked out in a way that she had no choice but to come out with him.

He took out the button from his pocket and opening Ramwati's palm he placed it in it. 'It is a diamond, Amma. Keep it carefully hidden. Don't let anyone know about it, not even the family. This is what she has left for you, for your old age.' He looked at the house. There was nobody at the door. Ramwati tucked the button into her blouse.

'He must have given it to her. Who gives a button to a girl?' she said.

Adhirath looked at Bharat.

'It was his. He must have given it to her and said that later he would get it turned into a ring,' said Bharat saving Adhirath the trouble of responding.

Taking her hand in his, Adhirath said, 'Ammaji, Parduman is guilty. But he is not the only one. That Udairaj is also guilty. Many more people are guilty. They exploited her. That pradhan and that ex-sarpanch, they too, and who knows who else. They did not kill her but what they did was also a crime. But they will not be punished.'

Ramwati's head was shaking. A small sob escaped her. She lifted her pallu to wipe her eyes.

'That crorepati will escape. There is only one way to bring him to justice. If some people in Delhi light candles at India Gate, if a lot of people light candles, perhaps then you can get some justice.'

Ramwati looked at him surprised. 'Beta you are very tired. You need rest.'

'No, Amma, this is the truth. Nobody lights a candle for the poor at India Gate.'

13

The month of May, the month of the blazing sun had arrived. Pushpa came to tell him that she has heard that her name is in the list of those promoted to the rank of Inspector. The list that had been made far back had not yet been announced. Even now the announcement was not official but it was expected to be made soon.

'Good. Very good. We must return the money we owe Nitesh,' he said.

'Will give him from this month's salary,' Pushpa said. The next day she handed him five thousand rupees.

'I was thinking I should also return Bapu's money from whatever little salary I get,' said Adhirath.

'What is the need?' Pushpa asked. 'Has he said anything? Tell me. Till now you never said you have to return his money.'

'I am no longer a dependent. So why should I be in his debt?'

'Is there something the matter?' Pushpa asked. She was annoyed.

'I told you: I don't feel good taking money from his small pension. You don't want to return what he lent? Keep this money then. I will get the entire amount from my bank,' he said handing back the money she had given him. 'Take your money back. I have enough. I will manage.'

Pushpa shrugged and said nothing. She knew this mattered to him. The loss of income makes a man feel less of a man and a woman should not hit him with her handsome salary. Relationships are fragile. They can break. Adhirath also knew that giving explanations all the time can snap ties however strong they may be. They can even break people. Only relationships define the identities of people.

Parduman was now in judicial custody. In prison. Nitesh took the money back after refusing it several times as was expected. On his way back, Adhirath felt the need to meet Udairaj. He found himself going to the club. There was a lot of hustle and bustle in the club. Garlands of flowers were looped around its doorways and the gate. Nobody at the reception was checking the guests to see who had come to see whom. Adhirath said to the man at the desk, 'Udairaj,' but before he could utter the word, the man extended a hand saying, 'Have you got the card, sir?'

'Card?'

'No problem. Will ask. A lot of people forget to bring cards. Some leave it in their cars.' He picked up the intercom and turned to Adhirath. 'Who should I say has come, sir?'

That is when a couple sauntered in, extracting a card from an envelope. The receptionist bent low and waved them onwards, saying 'First floor, sir.' The woman had a box, gift wrapped in a shiny paper.

'Saroj-ji will be here. I want to talk to her,' said Adhirath.

'Yes,' said the man, and then to the mouthpiece he said, 'Saroj Madam is there? What name should I tell her?' he asked Adhirath.

After five minutes he was on the first floor. Saroj met him at the door. Her kurta looked like waves of black sweeping over white, or was it the other way round? The churidar was black though, pitch black. Neither silk, nor cotton, something mixed, not glossy but how it glowed! She wore no dupatta. Flowers of the same dull white metal stuck to her ears and from each hung a single large pearl.

'I feel so happy to see you, that too, on my son's birthday,' she said with a smile. She sounded sincere.

'Sorry, I brought no present. I did not know.'

Saroj laughed. 'Come let me take you to meet my husband, my patidev,' she said with a faint trace of irony.

Udairaj was holding a Bloody Mary, but Adhirath's eyes were glued to his dark blue kurta. Three buttons winked at him from its buttonholes, diamonds on gold discs.

'You will have to have a drink today,' said Udairaj shaking hands with him.

'Your buttons are matchless,' said Adhirath.

'One button costs five lakhs,' said Udairaj.

'Each button! Are the diamonds so expensive?' asked Adhirath his eyebrows raised.

'Only one, the top one. The others are a little cheaper,' said Udairaj.

Adhirath turned to leave. Saroj followed him to the door.

'What happened to your job?' she asked.

'How do you know?' he asked. He was not surprised.

'You can get a lot of information for five lakhs. I did not call you that day. It was no use. He had three buttons. You might have guessed,' said Saroj. 'So what happened to the enquiry?'

'Madam, I may be about to lose my job,' said Adhirath.

Saroj walked with him to the door and said, 'Money has a lot of power. When the Jhandapuris got the support of money, they agreed to turn witnesses. If you had talked to me frankly, taken me into confidence...I did not know about the enquiry.'

Adhirath thought she was sad. She took out a small purse form the pocket of her kurta, a small pouch of white satin. Extracting a card from it, she handed it to him. 'I have started a business of interior decorations. Meet me some time. You are welcome at the farm too. Now it won't be sold.'

'May I ask you something?' asked Adhirath.

She bent her neck making it look like a question mark. Her brows shot up.

'Do you not feel scared? Living with a man like that?'

Saroj laughed. 'I live for my son. When I see his face, I feel no fear. Love teaches you to fight. To survive.'

Adhirath went down the stairs and looked up when he got to the bottom of the stairs. Saroj was still standing there looking at him. She was not smiling.

When he reached home a brown official envelope was on the table in the sitting room. It was open. He knew what the news was. Even so he slipped out the single sheet of paper in it and read it. He had been sacked. Dismissed from his job. He was to face trial. He inserted the paper back in the envelope.

'Arri bhaagwaan, you could have got some dahi,' he heard Daulatram's voice. Perhaps he had just got out of the bathroom inside.

'Get it now,' said Shakuntala.

'Now listen to her. The market may have closed by now.'

He looked up. Pushpa was standing in the doorway between the two rooms.

'The market is open,' Pushpa said.

ACKNOWLEDGEMENTS

The first word I must say is Thanks.

When Ravi Singh told me that he had asked Jerry Pinto to do the first edit of this translation of my novella, I was speechless with joy.

I have always admired Jerry for his prose and now I know what an accomplished editor he is. It reads better because of his diligence.

Thank you, Dyuti Roy, for doing the final edit so carefully and in double-quick time because I wished to be free earlier than you had planned.

Thank you, Ravi, for bringing Jerry and Dyuti in its life. It breathes easier now.